primer of **the novel**

books by **VINCENT McHUGH**

novels: TOUCH ME NOT

SING BEFORE BREAKFAST

CALEB CATLUM'S AMERICA

I AM THINKING OF MY DARLING

THE VICTORY

verse: THE BLUE HEN'S CHICKENS

primer of **the novel**

by **VINCENT McHUGH**

'Try to be one of the people on
whom nothing is lost.'

random house : new york

to my father

who taught me how to teach myself

foreword

THIS BOOK is perhaps not quite so simple as the title may indicate. It is a primer in the essential meaning of the term. It attempts to formulate certain 'elementary' principles and methods derived, for the most part, from the work of professional novelists of the first rank. We believe that this is the cardinal source for the study of what has been done and, by extension, what can be done in the novel. But since the novel is a somewhat advanced and complex art, its principles must be so too. We make them simple only at the risk of failing to qualify or modify; and in this broadest reach of fiction, if we fail in these matters we fail in all.

The book has been planned as a basic guide for the apprentice novelist, and for the student in intermediate or advanced writing classes, more especially in the field of adult education—the only field in which its author may claim some small competence as a teacher.

Even the working novelist may find that it will help to clarify his own methods, if only by dissent; and the rare and shining novel-reader who is concerned with such things may here get some account of what the novelist does and how he sets out to do it.

Each division of the book marks off a major aspect of the subject. Part One considers what may be called the propaedeutics (ungainly word) of the novel—those preliminary concepts on which it is built. Arranged by topics, this is in effect a series of extended definitions of the principal terms.

Part Two takes up the genetics of a particular novel—the whole process of conception, planning and writing, from the first hint to the finished Ms.

Part Three comprises a short natural history of the novelist—what he is like, how he lives, how much money he makes, and his relations with publishers, agents, editors, reviewers and his fellow novelists.

In the writing of this book, we have not been afraid of the obvious. The obvious is easily overlooked; and in an art so multifarious as the novel, it is best to take nothing for granted. Neither have we hesitated to use technical or other difficult terms whenever the exact sense called for them. A long word will sometimes do the work of five shorter ones. Moreover, we may assume that if the reader wishes to find out how a novel is written, or if he contemplates writing one himself, he will have developed enough verbal sophistication to be undismayed by such terms. If not, there is always the dictionary.

The chief disadvantage in a book of this kind is that, for the most part, it is condemned to be general; whereas the novel itself is forever particular. In Part Two, we have made some attempt to avert this difficulty by positing an imaginary novel. A book such as this is also required to dissociate elements—character, viewpoint, process, or whatever—which are in fact merely the various aspects of a given effect in the novel, and have no independent actuality. The attentive reader will note a good deal of what appears to be repetition. This is largely the associative restatement of a subject in its several aspects.

For much the same reason, we have deliberately used a rather small shelf of novels as versatile examples. The reader may familiarize himself with each novel and study it successively in terms of process, viewpoint or character. The more important of these novels, plus other titles, are mentioned in the combined list of references and sources at the back of the book. The interpolated numbers in the text refer to numbered titles in this list. Thus (26) denotes *The Art of the Novel,* by Henry James.

Here we may thank those students and other friends who prodded us to formulate one or another experiential principle and demanded that we should test it against the practice of the novelists they admired.

Beyond these matters, we may mention that this book is intended as a small act of devotion to the storyteller's great calling, and to that sense of tradition which makes us hope that those who come after us will somehow do better than we have done.

v . m c h .

contents

FOREWORD   vii

part one: the concepts

1 VOCABULARY   3
2 GENERAL AXIOMS   7
3 HISTORY   9
4 VEHICLES OF THE NOVEL   15
5 GENRES AND CATEGORIES   20
6 THE CHOICE OF SUBJECT   25
7 TYPES OF MATERIALS   30
8 THE USE AND TREATMENT
   OF MATERIALS   32
9 THE NOVEL'S RELATION
   TO THE WORLD   35
10 IMAGINATION   41
11 TIME: TENSE: DURATION:
   PACE: SIMULTANEITY   56
12 PROCESS   63
13 MODES OF PROCESS   77
14 THEMES   85

15 SYMBOLS   88
16 TONE AND KEY   90
17 RELATIVE SCALE   93
18 CHARACTER   96
19 DIALOGUE   106
20 NARRATIVE   108
21 VIEWPOINT   113
22 EXTENSION AND INTENSION   126
23 LEVELS OF MEANING   126
24 THE CONSCIOUS CONTROLS   128
25 THE UNCONSCIOUS
    SOURCES   131
26 ERRORS AND PITFALLS   135

part two: **the procedures**

1 GENERAL AXIOMS   141
 2 THE TOOLBOX   142
 3 PRIOR ATTITUDES   147
 4 THE HINT   150
 5 THE CONCEPTION   153
 6 THE FIRST OUTLINE   160
 7 THE TITLE   163
 8 THE RESEARCH   164
 9 THE GERMINATION   167
10 THE WORKING OUT OF
    THEMES   169
11 THE ARRANGEMENT OF
    SYMBOLS   171

12 THE DISCOVERY OF
PROCESS 175

13 PROCESS AS AN IMAGI-
NATIVE PROCEDURE 179

14 THE DISCOVERY OF
RELATIONS 183

15 SCENE AND CHARACTER 186

16 THE DEPLOYMENT OF
ELEMENTS 190

17 THE CALCULATION OF
STRESS AND PROPORTION 192

18 DRAWING UP THE MAJOR
OUTLINE 197

19 BLENDING THE ASSEMBLED
ELEMENTS 198

20 THE MAJOR OUTLINE AS AN
EXPERIMENTAL MODEL 199

21 THE MAJOR OUTLINE AS A
REFERENCE 201

22 THE ALLOWANCE FOR
IMPROVISATION 204

23 VARIANT TYPES OF
APPROACH 207

24 THE WRITING BEGINS 212

25 THE DAILY ATTACK 217

26 'THE STREAM OF COMPO-
SITION' 219

27 THE BLANK PERIOD 222

28 THE CONTROLLED RELAXA-
TION 224

29 REVISION AND REWRITING 227

30 THE APPLICATION AND RE-
LAXATION OF PRESSURES 233

31 THE FINISH LINE 235

32 THE REACTION 237

33 THE AFTEREFFECTS 241

part three: the novelist

1 GENERAL AXIOMS 249

2 THE PERSONALITY 251

3 THE SENSIBILITY 255

4 THE EDUCATION OF A
NOVELIST 258

5 THE NOVELIST AS A WRITER 265

6 ALTERNATIVE OR CON-
CURRENT OCCUPATIONS 266

7 THE WRITING REGIMEN 274

8 OCCUPATIONAL DISORDERS
OF THE NOVELIST 277

9 THE NOVELIST AS ARTIST 280

10 THE NOVELIST AS A BUSI-
NESS MAN 281

11 THE AUTHORS GUILD 283

12 THE AGENT 288

13 THE PUBLISHER 292

14 THE EDITOR   296
15 THE REVIEWER OR CRITIC   298
16 THE READER   300
17 THE REWARDS: PUBLIC
    AND PRIVATE   301

    REFERENCES   305

part one: **the concepts**

'. . . the germ of a theory is almost always the wish to prove what the theorist wishes to believe.' [51]

part one: the concepts

1 vocabulary

THE VOCABULARY of fiction-writing and the genetics of fiction, not to mention its criticism, is a horrible ragbag of words worn out with many uses, ambiguous and sliding terms, loose analogies loosely applied, and castoffs or borrowings from the other arts, from philosophy, science, journalism, rhetoric or whatnot. We have not tried to sort them out here. Neither have we tried to create a new and exact vocabulary—a job some philologist, in his mercy, ought to attempt. The howls of the novelists and critics will teach him quickly enough what should go into his revised edition. The short list below is intended (A) to limit the application of certain terms to their meanings in this book, and (B) to suggest a half-dozen neologisms made imperative by the hopeless ambiguity of older terms or the need of new words for new meanings.

autogenous process: a general type of organization that derives process from the particular subject and materials.

category: a traditional species of the novel, as the historical novel or the *roman philosophique,* usually classified in terms of form, subject or approach.

'conventional form': a type of process.

deployable time: any scheme that disposes of time segments out of their regular order, as flashbacks, etc.

disjunctive process: a type of process.

'dramatic treatment': Henry James's term. Treatment in developed and fronted scenes, as in a play—but not usually, of course, in play form.

duration: the total imaginary time span of a novel.

duration series: a succession of time panels separated by lapses of time, in consecutive or any arbitrary order.

element: any ingredient in a novel: theme, symbol, character, process, tone, etc.

foreshortening: condensed, summary narrative, in which much time-action is treated in a little space. Also, the strategy of such treatment.

imaginary time: the time convention of any novel.

key: pitch.

material: the percepts, facts, ideas, images, and other data converted and transfused into the novel.

'minor form': a type of process.

narrative bridge: a section of foreshortened narrative joining two scenes, the parts of a scene, or occurring at the beginning or end of a scene.

pace: the major tempo of a novel, comprising minor variations in tempo.

pattern: a configuration, used in a nontechnical sense.

'pictorial treatment': James's term again. Condensed or foreshortened narrative, especially as it is handled with a fresh immediacy.

process: any vehicle of development in the novel, from the structure of a sentence to 'the sense of the whole.' As a technical term, it is intended to comprise, with distinctions, the usage of *form, plot, composition,* etc. It is not in itself material, but a carrier of material.

proportion: the quantititative factor in emphasis, defined by its interrelations.

'qualitative progression': a type of process.

'repetitive form': a type of process.

running narrative: the major type of foreshortened narrative.

scene: developed and fronted treatment of a particular episode. Corresponds to 'dramatic treatment.'

straight narrative: narrative in the order of events as they might occur in time.

stress: the qualitative factor in emphasis.

style: minor form, determined by the tone and development required, plus the temperament of the writer.

subject: the story in its overt meaning—a small-town matron tries to realize her romantic wishes (*Madame Bovary*); a country parson takes charge of a blind girl and falls in love with her (*The Pas-*

toral Symphony); an older writer gives his young disciple certain ambiguous instructions in art and the rest of life (*The Lesson of the Master*).

'syllogistic progression': a type of process.

symbol: in the dictionary sense, as a token, a sign, 'something used or regarded as standing for something else.'

synergetic process: a type of combining process.

theme: (A) a concept translated into a particular and representative line of development; (B) 'the verbal parallel to a pattern of experience'; (C) a perceived line of growth emerging out of the material itself.

tone: the 'regularity of vibration' throughout a novel.

treatment: the major mode of handling the subject—i.e., naturalistic, comic, romantic, satiric, or any categorical or noncategorical alternative.

2 general axioms

There is really no such thing as *the* novel. The novel is always *a* novel—the specific problem, the particular case, the concrete instance.

A novel is a world in itself.

'A novel is a living thing, all one and continuous, like any other organism, and in proportion as it lives will it be found, I think, that in each of the parts there is something of each of the other parts.' [27]

A novel is always and forever people.

Could not a good novel be written about war in the ant colonies? Yes. We are dealing, not with rules, but with exceptionable principles.

A novel, said Stendhal, is 'a mirror dawdling down a road.'

'You must mix prose and poetry to get a good romance or even novel.' [41]

Nearly all writing *about* literature is a translation of its meanings from the primarily imaginative into primarily conceptual terms. It suffers the usual losses of translation and can only hope to make these good by supplying new planes of reference: historical, theoretical, procedural, critical, or whatever.

'The only obligation to which in advance we may hold a novel, without incurring the accusation of being arbitrary, is that it be interesting.' [27]

A novel cannot compete with direct sensation, and should not try. The heel of the loaf and a scooping of brook water are better food and drink than the dormice, nightingales, turtledoves and tamarisk wines of the banquet in *Herodias*.

'Where there is every freedom there is every license; and the novel, open-armed, free to all comers, claims more victims than the other forms of literature all put together.' [51]

Always and forever, the novel must concentrate on the particular, the specific: the cloud in the sky, the scar on the face, the ant under the leaf. If it does not do this first of all, it does not do anything.

3 history

Wherever anyone has told a long story, or a long series of connected stories, there the novel has been.

The novel is not a form. It is a medium capable of accommodating a great variety of forms.

What we call the novel is no handsome by-blow of the eighteenth or nineteenth century, sprung full-armed from the head of Lesage or Richardson or Stendhal or Flaubert. To maintain this, we should need to play the game of iron categories and assert a merely arbitrary—in this case, European-American—provincialism.

The novel must claim its great forbears.

Who told the cycles of the myths? Who made his listeners stare with the tales of Shiva, or the Prince of the Lonesome Island, or Actaeon hunted by his own dogs, or the Spider Woman of the Navajos? He was a novelist.

Who sat in his rags in all the marketplaces of the East, holding his half-moon of audience against the bustle of the traders, watching for the glint in his listeners' eyes and their quickened breath? Who drew them back the next day, and the next, with the intangible cord of his story? He too was a novelist.

Is a long story in verse less properly a novel because it is also poetry?

Great Homer and his *Odyssey,* 'with its well-knit plot, its psychological interest and its interplay of character, is the true ancestor of the long line of novels that have followed it.' [24]

And what of Herodotus, with his stories of the dead buried in honey, and of the women who served in the temple of Mylitta? [23] And Xenophon's *Cyropaedia,* which became the remote ancestor of

another significant name in the novel, Madeleine
de Scudéry's *Artamène, ou Le Grand Cyrus,* a monster in twenty volumes and twelve thousand pages?
[40] Or *Daphnis and Chloe,* with its thousand de-
scendants in the pastoral romance? Or the *Aethi-
opica* of Heliodorus, loved by the Elizabethans? Or
the *Satyricon* and *The Golden Ass* and Lucian's
True History? Are not all these out-and-out novels,
or a great deal more novel than creditable history?

Nor can we forget the Indian *Rāmāyanā,* or the
Panchatantra, or the *Vetāla.* We must claim, too,
the lost *Great Romance,* and *The Great Cluster of
Story,* and the *Ocean of the Rivers of Story,* and
the *Seventy Stories of a Parrot,* and *The Thirty-
Five Tales of Fools and Knaves.* [17]

Here we may see, in its beginnings, the gradual
coalescence of the story cycle into a unitary story
in which the whole is greater than its parts. The
evolution is traceable in several literatures. Its latter
phase has been isolated in the exclusive definition
of the novel as a single coherent and highly articulated web of narrative.

That is how we think of it at the midpoint of the
twentieth century. But the novel has been many
diverse things and will, no doubt, be quite other
things in the future. It would have taken an eerie
intelligence to predict *Finnegans Wake* as a remote
descendant of *Havelok the Dane.* How can we

guess what the grandchildren of such a novel as *Concluding* will be? [18]

At the time of the Mongol dynasty in China, the process of the coalescence of a series of tales into one long story was already well advanced. Besides the *Record of Travels in the West,* a novelist, presumably Lo Kuan-chung, had written *The Story of the Three Kingdoms,* which takes somewhat the same place in 'Chinese literature that *War and Peace* does in the Russian. Before the end of the seventeenth century A.D., China had produced such classic novels of love, or love-making, as the *Ch'in P'ing Mei* and the *Yü Chiào Li.* In the latter, an improbably Parisian triangle involving a student in love with two girls, we note the rather enviable latitude accorded to the Chinese novelist. The student marries both girls. [16]

In such instances, too, we may observe how much of the 'logic' of human relations is merely the set of a particular code of laws and customs. Such a code will vary, not only from culture to culture, but in each period of a culture. Thus, in *Diana of the Crossways,* Meredith's heroine becomes so disturbed over a divorce that we are inclined to regard her as an hysterical personality, whereas the reader of the 1970s may take her to be a more or less exact reflection of the social pressures in her time.

The good novelist will be well aware of these observances in his own and other cultures, but he will not hesitate to undercut or transcend them in his work.

Like the novel itself, the human situation is larger than any of its compartments.

The romance has been placed in one such compartment, walled off from the novel proper. But if we begin to set up exclusions, they will end by being endless. If we rule out *Aucassin and Nicolette*, the *Mabinogion*, the *Morte d'Arthur* and the other romances, by what sign shall we admit such odd fish as the *Gesta Romanorum*, the Italian *novellas*, *Gargantua* and *Pantagruel*, *The Princess of Clèves*, *Tristram Shandy* and *Wuthering Heights*? Is *Don Quixote* a satiric romance, or *Moby Dick* a philosophic one? And what is *Euphues* or *Oroonoko* or *Rameau's Nephew* or *Frankenstein* or *The Steel Flea* or *Ulysses* or *The Poet Assassinated* or *Portrait of the Artist As a Young Dog*?

No. We may conclude that the novel is a medium as large as the sea, and as little likely to be confined. It accepts the issue of every river and blends them all into its homogeneous blue.

But once we have said this, once we have made allowance for reversals and variations—the wild originals, the growth and decline of categories— we must grant the steady tendency of the novel, in nearly all literatures, toward a more intense consolidation and articulation of form. The parts become less and less salient in themselves, the old congeries of tales—so natural as the second phase of an art developed from the oral storytellers—tend to disappear in the inseparable process of the later novel.

This tendency has been dominant in the so-called art novel for at least a hundred years. The somewhat dandiacal pose of Stendhal failed to dissemble his relentless ordering of narrative. Balzac, who protested that he wrote only for money, developed the superb technical address of such a late novel as *Cousin Bette* largely as a practical economy of means. The groans of Flaubert at work echo down the century. Conrad's remark about Dostoevsky— 'That amateur!'—is the evidence of ten thousand hours spent at the task of bending the stiff and thorny brambles of experience into some meaningful imaginative pattern. In James the horror of looseness became an acute moral rorce. Stephen Crane, his polar opposite as an American novelist, could write narrative with the apocalyptic frugality of a telegrapher reporting a wreck on the line. Some of Gide's earlier novels have the structure of a butterfly's wing seen against the light; and Mann's *Death in Venice* displays the austere development of a perfect small musical form.

We may note how this movement toward the more intense organization of the novel is carried to its

stylized extreme of mannerism in the work of such
diverse popular writers as Hammett and Mar-
quand. Here a few parts from the immense stock
of formal principles have been fitted together into
a simple machine that runs with commendable
speed and precision—if we do not ask what has
been left out, or what it will not do.

Will the curve of this long-term tendency toward
formal organization project itself into the future?
Perhaps not, or at least not in the sense we have
known it. This is not to say that formal process
will go by the board. On the contrary, it is likely
to be put to new and more complex uses. The ambiguous symbol, multiple levels of meaning, an
enlistment of the patterns of dream and myth, the
unresolved human action, and perhaps chiefly a
sense that the human personality and the objective
action are both far more limitless and fluid than we
had supposed:—all these will call for a virtuosity
hitherto unexplored in the novel.

The term *novel* derives from the Latin diminutive
for *new*. Who will do what new thing next?

4 vehicles of the novel

We may assume that the ancestors of the novel, in
myth or folk stories or travelers' accounts, were all
tales told directly by a narrator to a listening audience.

But we have become so accustomed to the novel produced by letterpress that we can hardly imagine it in any other guise.

'If it be true that the printed book is only the manuscript stereotyped, it is equally true that the manuscript is only the spoken word committed to writing.' [44]

In the main, perhaps, but not quite. The oral storyteller has at his disposal a whole battery of voice inflections and kinesthetic intimations, plus the orator's or the actor's interplay with his audience. These will be lost, or must be supplied in other ways, when the story is reduced to print. The more or less silent visual word displaces the oral one.

But other things are gained. The novelist in print may count on a good deal more latitude in patience and time. He is addressing a single auditor rather than a presumable group. He can hope, at least, for a good deal more indulgence in the way of subtleties, thorough development, time changes, and indirect narrative.

But the principle of the omnipresent narrator—the storyteller himself, or his one or a dozen interposed surrogates—is still the unique principle that distinguishes fiction from all the other arts.

How is it that the drama has established a kind of priority of method in such vehicles as the motion picture, radio, television, even disc recording? Is it a better storytelling device than the novel? In certain respects, yes. It can embody and enact a scene. The novel can only project it, though the resources of the novel make it possible to do more, and more kinds of things, with a scene than the drama can. We may grant, too, that the dramatic method is much better suited to the larger audiences of the stage and the motion picture.

The drama is a public art, and the motion picture, at least as it has been used commercially, is essentially a public medium. This public effect—even in Shakespeare, or Racine, or Sophocles—is intended to strike the common chord in a large number of people, and is thus somewhat coarse and overbold in its appeal to the individual.

The art of the narrator is a private art, addressed in each instance to one or a few people.

So far as storytelling goes, the radio, television, and disc, wire or tape recording are all basically private media. There is no such thing as 'the radio audience.' That is rank mysticism. There are only innumerable separate auditors, or groups of a dozen or less, who happen to be listening simultaneously. This distinction applies even more closely to the other vehicles mentioned.

Thus the art of the narrator, as a private art, is particularly well suited to radio, television, and electronics recording.

But how shall we translate the novel into forms appropriate to these media? The question contains a number of fallacies. One is that translation will be necessary. Another is that translation implies dramatization. A third is that the medium dictates the form. None of these is true, or true only in minor respects.

The type of reproduction does not and should not determine the narrative form, though it may modify this form.

What we mean to suggest is that the novelist may write directly for radio or television, for microgroove or tape recording, as he has so long written directly for letterpress. But he will write *as a novelist*—a teller of long tales. He will everywhere maintain the dominant principle of the narrator—though he himself, of course, may not be the explicit narrator. But he will reclaim, in effect, his basic role as the oral storyteller.

We must concede at once that the transience of radio and television programs, plus their fixed conventions and the other terms on which they operate, make them practically unavailable to the novel. If they are to be reached at all, they must be reached by means of films and recordings which can enlist their own multiple small audiences. We may imagine the 'opening night' of a novel on radio, the first presentation of a work that will be released to the public next day in books and records.

The most promising new avenues for the novel lie
open in recordings—wire, tape or disc—and in the
home motion-picture projector using 8- or 16-milli-
meter film. For these vehicles, production costs will
be small. Manufacturing conditions in the middle
of the twentieth century made it seem likely that
disc records might be able to compete with the cost
of books. Reproduction costs in the other media
—film, and wire or tape recordings—were still high
enough to suggest marketing primarily in terms of
rental rather than sales.

Just as printing modified the techniques of the oral
storyteller, so these new vehicles will call for an
imaginative adaptation to their limits and possibilities. The novelist will discover fresh ways and
means. He will certainly move toward shorter time
segments. Like the dramatist, he will enlist the resources of the other arts: music and sound effects
for records, plus decoration, color, and visual devices for the intimate motion picture.

But even in the motion picture, his story will not
be acted out. He will hew to his main line: the
voice of the narrator, speaking with imaginative intensity of certain events that might be true. Thus
he will gain, like the novelist in print, an invaluable
focus within the work itself. He will have his mobile
angle of vision. He will have his principle of selection and coherence. He will be free to move into
all the areas of human personality—at the farthest

outset of objective vision, or in the deepest wells of the psyche. And always he will have at his disposal the invaluable persuasion of the human voice, speaking—out of the center of personality and imagined experience—of things seen and known and suffered.

5 genres and categories

'I? A crustacean?' said the crab in William James's fable. 'No, by God! I am myself. Myself alone.'

Every good novel is *sui generis*. It is itself. Itself alone.

There are as many possible varieties of novels as there are genuinely original minds to create them— or more, since one truly imaginative writer may introduce a dozen genres.

But 'the literary kind is not a mere name, for the aesthetic convention in which a work participates shapes its character.' [47] Or we may say, more precisely, that no matter how original a work may be, the category still exerts some modifying influence as a tradition. The novelist must take stock of this, and acknowledge or discount it.

Categories will tend to become more prominent in classicist or other traditionalist periods; or perhaps in periods during which social relationships are comparatively fixed; or during periods in which the critical sense becomes more powerful than the creative force in literature.

Categories will tend to die out (except as labeled commodities—the mystery story, for example) in unsettled social periods, or in periods during which each writer concentrates most intensely on making his novel an individual work. This procedure in turn may create new categories.

All genres and categories appear to be subject to the usual morphology of conventional forms. They grow prominent, die out, and sometimes reappear in other guises. They are capable of many mutations and symbioses.

Categories are (A) types of 'conventional form,' in Kenneth Burke's definition [3]; (B) a stressing of the traditional element in a work, and thus a promise of literary recognition, which appeals to us in somewhat the same way that the exact repetition of a story appeals to a child; (C) more or less loose conveniences for literary historians, critics, publishers and readers.

Categories may be classified primarily as to form (the Italian *novellas,* the mystery story); as to subject, or type of material (the sea story, the war story, the scientific novel); or in terms of the novelist's approach (the philosophic, or religious, or topical novel).

We may list a few of the more traditional categories. Some of the examples given should perhaps be followed by question marks.

(A) *The Picaresque.* This is generally understood to derive from the picaroon romance of Spain, a tale of wandering rogues or vagabonds, usually at odds with the society in which they find themselves. This basic definition has been extended to mean any story of wandering adventures. It is evident that the genre itself is much older than the term. Historically it bears a resemblance to one of the four main divisions of the Chinese novel—a tale of 'brigandage and lawless characters generally,' as Giles [16] defines it. Thomson, in a pointed anachronism, describes the *Satyricon* as 'a satire in the form of a picaresque novel.' [44] Examples: *Gil Blas, The Unfortunate Traveller, Jonathan Wild, Adventures of Huckleberry Finn, Lafcadio's Adventures.*

(B) *The Novel of Village or Country Life.* Examples: Balzac's *The Country Doctor; The Village,* by Ivan Bunin; *A Nest of Simple Folk; The House by the Medlar Tree.*

(C) *The Roman Philosophique.* Examples: Xenophon's *Cyropaedia; Utopia; Candide;* Mann's Joseph trilogy; *The Root and the Flower,* by L. H. Myers.

(D) *The Young Girl's Story.* This is not a well-recognized genre, perhaps because it so often goes over into the romance; but its line is distinct in continental, English and American literature. Examples: Marivaux's *Marianne; Pamela;* Madame de Stael's *Corinne; Manon Lescaut;* Rousseau's *Julie; Lamiel; Mademoiselle de Maupin; Daisy Miller.*

(E) *The War Novel.* This had an early development in Chinese literature; but as a distinct category, it emerged rather late in Western European and American usage. Examples: Tolstoy's *Sevastopol,* some of the novels of Erckmann and Chatrian, *The Chouans, Miss Ravenel's Conversion, The Red Badge of Courage, The Enormous Room, Three Soldiers, A Farewell to Arms, Quiet Flows the Don, All Thy Conquests.*

(F) *The Regional Novel.* This may be defined as a novel of provincial life which emphasizes the peculiarities of a region rather than its universal aspects. Examples: *The House of the Seven Gables;* Amado's *The Violent Land;* Bandelier's *The Delight-Makers;* Trollope's *The Vicar of Bullhampton.*

(G) *The Romance.* Among the various meanings of this term we may indicate (A) a story in the general mode of Chrestien de Troyes or *Aucassin and Nicolette;* (B) the *roman d'aventure,* from *Apollonius of Tyre* and *Havelok the Dane* to *The Wanderer* and *The Arrow of Gold;* (C) the love story per se; (D) a kind of story that claims, in tone and treatment, a special dispensation from the probable

—an indulgence perhaps closer to fable than to poetry or fantasy.

We may also note in passing such categories as the Gothic novel, the satire, the novel of social criticism, the historical novel, the scientific novel, the novel of manners, the collective novel and the comic novel.

There is another and broader category: that which distinguishes between the novel as literature and the novel as popular entertainment. This is perhaps a necessary convenience at times, but too arbitrary to be taken seriously. The extremes are clear enough. But any novel may have some of the qualities of literary art. It would be hard to lay down a dividing line, or a zone of division; and even if we did so, would we not thereby cut the umbilical between a popular novel and the work or type of literary art from which it derived? The American Western story, for example, is a *roman d'aventure* crossed with the regional novel.

It is perhaps more useful to follow Kenneth Burke in the sense that all novels are literature. Once we have done this we shall be free to assign a particular work its point of valuation on the scale.

According to the horrible practices of literary terminology, *genre, category* and *type* are often used interchangeably. *Genre*, however, has another definition in criticism, French criticism in particular. It may mean a pure and limpid story of simple lives, and is thus very close to the sense of pastoral.

Genres and categories must be distinguished from the great basic themes: the journey, the quest, death and resurrection, going home, the seven labors of the hero, and so on.

6 the choice of subject

Perhaps no aspect of the novel has been so often underestimated as the importance of the choice of subject.

A novel may be *about* anything: the mutual approach of two stars in their orbits, or the approach, collision and destruction of two star-crossed lovers.

Everything in the actual universe and the universe of the imagination is a fit subject for the novel—if the novelist is man enough.

The importance of the choice of subject involves, but must be distinguished from, the relative social or topical interest of the story itself. Thus a novelist who would make a very thin affair out of panoramic war in North Africa (broad social interest) might be intensely moving in his account of a Cajun girl's love for her pet heron (narrow social interest).

Theoretically the professional novelist ought to be able to undertake any subject with the assurance that he will turn out a sound piece of work—though he will be more successful with some subjects than others. A few professional novelists, making skilful use of research, simplification and selection, have actually approached this standard.

Practically speaking, however, an apt choice of subject must take account of certain limiting factors.

(A) What has been done before, how often and how well it has been done, and what kinds of treatment it has been given. A novelist of the 1950s who sets out to do a New England town has a stiff row to hoe. He must consider the work of Hawthorne, Henry James, John W. De Forest, Edith Wharton, Mary E. Wilkins Freeman, Thomas Bailey Aldrich, Jonathan Leonard, Robert Frost, Eugene O'Neill, Thornton Wilder, and how many others? His subject has been dealt with as romance, naturalistic tragedy, symbolic tragedy, quaint comedy, satire, gnomic poetry, and in a dozen other ways. Moreover, it is a subject that calls for the most minute knowledge of local character and mores in a traditionally tight and guarded society. He must ask himself whether it is worthwhile to try it again. Can he do something fresh with it? Certainly the task is not impossible. But it will require a new intensity in the particular, a new angle of vision, perhaps an untouched kind of incidence between New England and the larger world.

A well-worked tradition, relatively narrow and un-
diverse, may handicap the novelist quite as much
as a broader and ampler tradition would aid him.

(B) The sensibility of any novelist is not, after all,
unlimited—though he may never have developed
his full range. He may just possibly be able to carry
off a subject at the extreme margins of his temperament. But why should he, when he can choose another that will provide the happiest conjunction
between temperament and story?

Flaubert took an even stricter view. The novelist,
he wrote, 'does not choose his subject. This is something that the public and the critics do not comprehend, but the secret of all masterpieces lies in the
concordance between the subject and the temperament of the author.' [14]

Must we suppose then that his subject chooses him?
Sometimes, and in a certain sense. But a novelist
who knows his own aptitudes and temperament
should—indeed, must—select a subject that will fit
him.

The better he knows himself and his subject, the
better the work is likely to be. This is the sense in
the usual counsel to a young writer that he should
write 'only about what he knows.' The nonsense is
that (A) he may be too much involved with what
he knows to make anything objective out of it; (B)

what he knows may not suit his temperament or his aptitudes; (c) he may be finished with what he knows, the aliveness gone out of it for him; and (d) something quite beyond his own experience may prick his imagination in ways that the familiar could never do.

The case of the mature professional is somewhat different, though perhaps only in degree. He knows more about himself and his craft, and he is less at the mercy of what he does not know about human experience. He may light on a subject about which he is almost completely ignorant; but if it strikes him hard enough, he will know how to find out about it. Before he wrote *Salammbo,* Flaubert went to North Africa to look at the old sites of Carthage. James prowled the back quarters of London to catch 'the Tone' he needed for *The Princess Casamassima.* But whereas Flaubert read hundreds of books and climbed through the whole archaeology of his period, James insisted (as always) that very little was enough for the imagination and that too much would drown the ominous intimation he wished to convey. [26]

(c) A subject unworkable for a particular novelist in one kind of treatment may, in another kind, be just what he requires. Thus a writer who might be unable to manage a story about the Spanish settlement of Florida in terms of historical incident may do very well with it as rococo fantasy.

Perhaps the highest and most legitimate virtuosity of the professional is called out (A) by a subject that will give play to the whole range and diversity of his talent, and (B) by the effort to project this same subject in a kind of treatment best suited both to its inherent possibilities and to the writer's own temperament. This is not to make the same point twice. A subject beautifully adapted to a writer's talent may somehow leave him cold.

The relative social or topical interest of a subject will, of course, have a major bearing on the number of readers who will accept it, and the intensity of their acceptance. In the United States, certain subjects are notorious reader-bait: physical love-making, the rationalization of religion, a somewhat infantile preoccupation with the breasts of the human female, nostalgia for the crinoline past, the romanticism of the big city, violence with a gun or other penis substitute, etc. In certain European countries, an infantilism obsessed with tenuous philosophies and the uneasy backwaters of the psyche may at times take the place of the American sensational infantilism.

The topical subject (When will the Houyhnhnms make war? Should a girl wear pantalettes when she dresses for dinner?) is always marked with a time stop. It claims a premium on the immediate, and this premium is voided when the immediate lapses.

Certain novelists may exploit the sensational or topical aspects of a subject for commercial or other reasons—including some perfectly good ones. This does not mean that such subjects, in themselves, are closed to the serious writer. But he must evaluate and discount the sensational or topical factors; and this requires, in general, an extended perspective and a new depth of insight.

The opposite mistake is a good deal more common, and perhaps even more regrettable. A serious writer will avoid subjects he is quite capable of treating because he confuses the 'major' with the 'obvious,' and the 'obvious' with the 'popular.'

A subject may be inadvisable for all but the most scrupulous craftsman simply because it is unrewarding in itself or because it has been worn out by other writers.

But no subject, per se, is either 'serious' or 'popular.' All that depends on the treatment chosen and the degree of skill expended on it.

7 types of materials

Nothing could be less 'material' than the materials of the novelist. They are, almost by definition, intangibles.

The smell of hay fresh-cut in the salt marshes; the weird rolling of tumbleweeds in the gloom of a dust storm; the soft cosmos colors of dresses revolving and spreading in the glitter of a ballroom; the faroff mutter of big naval rifles addressing an island: —all these are 'materials.'

The soft enveloping urgency of love-making in a dream; the multiple apparition of Coleridge's moon at Keswick, 'supported by *the images of memory flowing in on the impulses of immediate impression*' [30]; the hallucinations of cerebral malaria, or those of business ambition; Dos Passos's accurate and remote association between the smell of wine and the smell of wet sawdust; or lights, voices, gusts of emotion, fantasies, airs of music, coming fresh out of the imagination when we had not known they were there: —these too are 'materials.'

A friend's story about prospecting for uranium; an article in the *American Journal of Psychology;* a technical study of sympathin; a page from the Chinese philosopher Chuang Chou; the account of a small-boat voyage to Antigua; William Bartram's immortal *Travels;* a newspaper clipping about shale oil: —these are 'materials' also.

Thus we may define three roughly practical but by no means mutually exclusive orders of material: (A) the direct experience of the writer's senses; (B) experiences evolved out of memory, eidetic images, dreams, the unconscious—the interior imagination in general; and (C) conceptual or factual materials

—the selective abstractions of philosophy, law, medicine, journalism, physics, or whatever.

8 the use and treatment of materials

'It is what the artist does with his materials, not where he gets them, that is the question.' [41]

Economy is not in itself a virtue, nor prodigality a vice. Nevertheless, in the novel, there are many more spendthrifts than misers.

The seeds of whole books have been thrown away in an unconsidered paragraph.

But the full use of material does not denote the inclusion of every last detail related to it. The material itself is inert, undifferentiated, and at best fragmentary matter. Like every other element in the novel, it demands selection. This selection must serve the requirements of a particular novel and the particular subject, treatment, viewpoint, key, etc., chosen for it. That is the principle of selection.

The data available on any given phenomenon are theoretically infinite, and infinitely extensible. A crowd gathers to watch a warehouse fire. In the crowd are men and women of many callings. A reporter phones in what he thinks of as 'the facts.' His 'facts' are merely the selection of data he has

been trained to make. The fire chief notes that
Engine Company 2 is moving its hoses into the
right position to block off the flames and sends
Engine Company 4 to support it. A religious person
in the crowd thinks of the fires of hell. A detective
knows that the owners of the building have been
close to bankruptcy, and wonders if the fire was set.
A chemist observes the color of the flames and de-
duces that copper paint must have been stored in
the building. A pest-control man reflects that the
rats will move into the adjoining warehouses. An
artist muses on the involved pattern of hoses in
the street. A physicist considers the release of gases
and their behavior in the upper atmosphere. Into
the imagination of a poet comes the notion that
these windy flames are like palms in a hurricane.
Moved by the pleasant excitement, a man in the
crowd speaks to a pretty girl and walks away with
her.

If we expand this crowd into a multitude composed
of specialists in every phase of human awareness,
and if we then persuade each specialist to carry his
observations as far as he can, we shall have some
idea of the kinds and amount of data potentially
available on any casual event. All of this is presumably at the service of the novelist who knows what
to do with it. No novelist born of woman will attempt to use one-tenth of one per cent of it; but that
small portion, within the chosen terms of his fiction,
must suggest the whole.

Thus the novelist's device of selection must be regarded as a kind of abstraction, too. But he differs from the scientist or the philosopher in that he selects in order to reconstitute the living 'sense of the whole,' as a cartoonist arranges a series of dots to suggest the single line of a profile. (In passing, we may note the parallel beginnings of the concern for a 'sense of the whole' in physiology, psychosomatic medicine, Gestalt psychology, and ecology.)

This brings us to a second tentative axiom governing the use of materials in the novel. The selected materials, chosen with a view to the particular subject and treatment, should be exploited to the full. This means that they must be rolled in the hand, turned upside down and inside out, combined and re-combined, until every facet catches the light. The alert reader will expect all the relevant aspects of an event to be balanced and accounted for; but more than that, the novelist, by exhausting the properties of his material, will hope to discover the fullest possible system of relationships between events in the book.

We have defined treatment as 'the major mode of handling the subject—i.e., naturalistic, comic, romantic, or whatever.' But it is not, of course, merely categorical. The more original the book, the less likely is the chance that its treatment will be definable even in terms of the multiple seriocomic amalgamation of categories.

It is determined by, and itself helps to determine, the other elements in the novel—subject, key, themes, viewpoint, scale, and so on. Thus in a novel about the Civil War, philosophic in theme, related by a very old woman as a childhood memory, and in a somewhat brooding tone, we should hardly expect a treatment in terms of the crackling slang of the 1920s. But even this is conceivable in a broadly comic handling of the same subject, by the same narrator. In that case the themes would become satiric rather than philosophical, the key higher, the tone somewhat raucous. Moreover, we should require an almost totally different kind of material. An incident suited to the philosophic theme would be grotesque in terms of the satirical. Thus we may assume that the influence of treatment on the choice and use of materials tends to be decisive.

9 the novel's relation to the world

There is no such thing as fact in a novel. In fiction, all is fiction.

Certain statements in a novel may be 'factually' verifiable, but the point is irrelevant. Their operational value is not factual. They are there for other reasons: to create, as in the novels of Defoe, an *effect* of the factual; to establish a comfortable recognition or belief in the reader; to discount incredulity about more fantastic events; because they will serve the purpose better than wholly imaginary details; or, more generally, because the writer, having chosen a certain scene or subject, is committed to some degree of correspondence with the actual. Thus, if a novelist has named Fifth Avenue in New York, he must not place it next to Park Avenue or Fourth Avenue. But if he has merely mentioned 'a great avenue that lifts northward out of a small green square,' he may do what he likes with it.

Even when an actual city, Paris, or an actual ocean, the Pacific, is mentioned, it must still be created largely as if it had never been. Indeed, when an existent place is named, as Henry James pointed out in discussing the mistakes he had made in *Roderick Hudson* [26], the novelist incurs severer demands, and limits himself far more than if he had chosen to represent an imaginary locale. We may see the errors of *Roderick Hudson* triumphantly reversed in *The Ambassadors,* where the faroff rumor of an imaginary town, Woollett, Massachusetts, makes an essential counterpoint to the action in Paris.

This problem is not solely a matter of the reader's knowledge or recognition. It involves the whole question of the casually topical in literature—even when the book is not a topical novel. Moreover, it is a problem that concerns both time and place, sometimes inextricably. The difficulty extends even to matters of detail. Is it to the novelist's advantage to use the actual names of streets, bars, hotels and other public places in a city? Should he also denominate the songs, personalities, topical jokes and news event of a period?

We may certainly say yes in the case of such designed period novels as Flaubert's *Sentimental Education,* Dos Passos's *U. S. A.* or Romains's *Men of Good Will.* In taking a period as their subject, as the thing to be projected, they escape for the most part being merely *of* a period—i.e., period pieces. But there are other kinds of novels. It is difficult to conceive even the most tentative principle here. Exceptions fly up on every hand. We may suggest that matters of general knowledge— Grand Central Terminal, the Golden Gate Bridge, Whitehall, the Eiffel Tower and so on—are unexceptionable. Beyond that point judgment must rule. The chance of recognition is not enough. The novelist must *make* his effect of place as he would make any other. Naming is not creating.

Novels which exploit the fashions of a period—in speech, food, drinks, ideas, places—will suffer the usual fluctuations of the modish. *Avant-garde* when they appear, they will be inexpressibly dated in five years, but may rise again in fifteen or twenty, first as period revivals and later, if they have merit, as serious work. We may see the end phase of this cycle in many of the minor Elizabethan and Restoration comedies. Their fashionable references, long since obscured, have an allusive piquancy that transcends the notes with which they are all too often loaded.

But the novelist has larger matters to deal with. His book, conceived as an autonomous world, is yet *in* the world, and will act upon it—that is, on the reader. By the same token, it is subject to the various reactions of its world. Kenneth Burke has long since made this subject his province, and we may quote a few of his formulations and examples [3]. (Burke uses the term 'Symbol' to indicate symbolic pattern in literature; we have chosen to employ 'symbol' in its more basic meanings.)

Such a pattern, he writes, 'is perhaps most overwhelming in its effect when the artist's and the reader's patterns of experience closely coincide,' *Childe Harold* is cherished by 'mute Byrons.' Patterns of this kind may also, he suggests, appeal: (A) 'as the interpretation of a situation' (*Babbitt*); (B) 'by enabling the acceptance of a situation' (*The Grapes of Wrath*); (C) 'as the corrective of a situation' (*Treasure Island,* read by a boy who finds school dull); (D) 'as the exerciser of "submerged" experience' (sadism in a historical novel), and so on. The examples are ours. We might adduce even more striking instances—the conclaves of women who wept over readings of *Adolphe,* or the chain of suicides apparently touched off by *The Sorrows of Young Werther*.

These are a few of the ways in which the patterns
of a novel may have their effect on the reader. Some
of these may be planned, of course, some entirely
unconsidered. In either event, they are well worth
the most intense scrutiny any novelist can give
them.

But the larger world in which the novel has its being will also react on it, sometimes in odd ways. We
know the simpler ones. A book may do well, or
badly, or so-so. A sudden change in reading tastes
may leave an excellent novel stranded; or some
minor aspect of a good novel may spread it out to
a large public. In general, the known commodities
will do the calculated things. The careers of other
books will be no more predictable than a turn at
roulette.

There are, however, more significant factors having
to do with the whole social climate: current or
long-term attitudes, ideas and living ways. Sexual
treatment of a kind that would not have got past
an American publisher's door in the 1880s (unless,
of course, it happened to be the work of a French
writer) was wholesomely current, though not always unchallenged, at the outset of the 1950s.
Again, at the approach of war in the early 1940s,
many Americans set out to read *War and Peace*—
partly, perhaps, because it had been furnished with
a brilliant new historical introduction by Clifton
Fadiman, but largely too out of admiration for the

Russian armies and their tradition. By 1947 this admiration had darkened into apprehension; and a novel written in praise of Russian military power would have had, at best, only a horrified audience, plus perhaps an infinitesimal covey of sympathizers.

These social reactions on the novel may be of many kinds. For example, criticism of the power exercised by women, as a group, in American society is notoriously quick death to a novel; whereas the 'beautiful and unscrupulous woman' in fiction has become so much of a cliché that she may almost be regarded as a social ideal. But a burlesque of this type might be less welcome. Again, we have seen how a minority cause, equal social rights for Negro people, may become a dominant—a professed dominant, at least—in our culture. In this case, even when there was no intent to create propaganda, the novel played a considerable role. It acted strongly and was strongly acted upon.

Novels of the first order will, of course, take account of these social divergences and transcend them in a grasp for 'universals.' In such a novel, a talented Negro physicist, working with the dangerous ore of uranium in its peaceful uses, may be trapped at the beginning of his career by the accident of his color. But his meaning will surmount time and place and color. He will be Prometheus, chained to his rock and gnawed by the vulture, waiting for the hand of Hercules to set him usefully free in the world again.

10 imagination

'Imagination,' said a psychologist, 'is the point at which all the systems of psychology go over the cliff.'

We shall attempt to take up its workings, for the specific use of the novelist, in other places. Here we are concerned with the task of trying to find out *how* it works—at least in what appears to be its major phase. If the novelist can learn to guide and influence this phase to some extent, he may well leave the final definition of imagination to the critics, psychologists, semanticists and lexicographers. Life is short, and he has other fish to fry.

He will agree, however, that a little knowledge of what I. A. Richards calls 'the originative facts of mind' may perhaps be of use to him. Let us begin with the dictionary. [1B] Under *imagination,* it gives 'the action of imagining, or of forming mental images or concepts,' etc., and 'the *faculty* of forming such images or concepts.' *Concepts* here should be understood in the sense of both *ideas* and *data.* The dictionary supplies a third meaning: 'the *power* of reproducing images stored in the memory under the suggestion of associated images (reproductive imagination) or of recombining former experiences in the creation of new images different from any known by experience (productive or creative imagination).' It adds two more relevant to our purposes: 'the faculty of producing ideal creations consistent with reality, as in literature (distinguished from fancy)' and 'a conception or mental creation, often a baseless or fanciful one'—i.e., the playful or pathological issue of the imagination.

We need not criticize these in detail. It is enough to note (A) the variety of materials said to be acted upon by the imagination—images, image clusters, concepts (ideas and data), experiences, and perhaps hallucinations. Together they comprise nearly all the materials available to human consciousness, except perhaps what are loosely called 'the emotions'; and certainly emotion can hardly be dissociated from 'experiences' or the imagination. (B) In regard to the faculty itself, we have been given descriptions rather than definitions. These tell us what it *does,* not what it *is.* Nor is a good dictionary alone in this.

What is *imagination,* then? We may begin by suggesting that it is either a term which has been applied to too many disparate actions, or that there is an operative kinship between these actions. Anyone who has considered the works of Leonardo da Vinci, projected or accomplished—a painting, a bridge, an architectural plan, a piece of music, a statue, a mathematical formula, a helicopter, a machine gun, the aphoristic notebooks, a parachute, the discovery of the rings of annual growth in exogenous trees, a naval architect's drawing—will have suspected a common process at work in the whole. This word *genius* is less an explanation than a disclaimer. All of us show signs of Leonardo's versatility, though usually at a much lower point in the scale; and those of us who do not may well have blocked it off in the intense pursuit of some specialized activity.

These signs in themselves are enough to suggest the possibility that what is variously called 'the imagination' or 'the creative faculty' or 'the germinative principle' or 'the creative unconscious' is not a distinguishable faculty at all—historically the classic presumption, in one form or another. It may be that imagination is purely a sequence of procedures, a way of doing things, a 'natural' syllogism corresponding to the 'invented' syllogism of logic. It is perhaps a kind of *modus operandi* potentially available and common to all the fields of human intelligence. We may, if we like, think of it as a fixed numerical series that will perhaps open the combination lock of any safe (a valuable invention for the safecracker). The 'safe' may be a problem or project of whatever kind—a novel, a tentative mathematical concept, a sonata, a bridge, the purification of an antibiotic, a point of mystical belief, or the deployment of salesmen in new territory. If it is not solvable, entirely or in part, by ordinary thinking (which may contain imaginative elements too), or by rote—that is, by means of solutions pre-

viously thought or imagined, tested and found satisfactory—then it is almost certain to require the intervention of the imaginative procedure.

There is a good deal of evidence—scattered and
somewhat nebulous, but extraordinarily suggestive
—to document the hypothesis that imagination is
not a distinct faculty but a kind of organic series of
the intelligence, applicable to a variety of materials.
Or perhaps we should merely suggest this as the
major phase of imagination. But aside from the
work of Coleridge, Galton, Ribot, Jung and a few
others, the difficulty with most of this evidence is
that it has been formulated by psychological ama-
teurs, usually prominent in some other field, who
have been moved to consider the operations at
work in their discoveries. For the same reason, however, these observations have a fresh credibility untouched by *a priori* notions or frames of reference.
Usually they are not 'investigations.' Indeed, they
have most often been set down because their authors were surprised into recognition of processes
they could not account for.

Moreover, we have, in many instances, an excellent
check, compromised only by a rather disappointing
unawareness, even among artists, as to the nature
of the imaginative process. About a poem by
Baudelaire or a piece of program music by Res-
pighi, opinions may differ somewhat, though most
critics will be in general agreement. Other cases

are clearer. Henry James regarded *The Ambassa-dors* as his best long novel, and not many critics of the novel would disagree with him. Evidence of this kind, however, would not carry much weight among engineers or biologists, though they might defer to expert opinion in a field in which they lacked competence. But a bridge imagined and built, a bridge that answers all demands on it, from peak traffic load to esthetics; or a mathematical theorem triumphantly elegant and applicable; or the solution of a problem in biochemistry, tested in the laboratory and subsequently found effective in whole populations:—each of these is a 'fact of great yield,' as Poincaré said, and capable of satis-fying the most skeptical mind. It is evident, in many cases, that the imaginative series helped to bring about these results; but we may not therefore con-clude that it is the *only* method competent to do so. We shall see, in fact, that it is perhaps merely an in-tegrant, though the key one, in a combination of methods.

We may cite a few examples, chosen for their di-versity. Setting 'fancy' aside, Coleridge distin-guishes between two orders of imagination. He mentions 'the primary Imagination' as the 'prime Agent of all human Perception,' and goes on to define 'the secondary Imagination . . . as an echo of the former, co-existing with the conscious will, yet still as identical with the primary in the *kind* of its operation. It dissolves, diffuses, dissipates, in order to recreate; or where this process is rendered impossible, yet still at all events it struggles to idealize and to unify. . . .' [38] We may, for our purposes, take Coleridge's 'primary Imagination' simply as perception in all its aspects and combinations, and his 'secondary Imagination' as the thing we are dealing with.

So much for the poet's experience, thoroughly discussed by I. A. Richards [38] and John Livingston Lowes [30], among others. Now let us consider the mathematician's. Hadamard [21] cites one incident, among others, mentioned by Henri Poincaré. Poincaré had interested himself in Fuchsian functions and 'attacked the subject vainly for a fortnight,' trying at first to prove that such functions did not exist. Not succeeding in this, he managed, during a sleepless night, to construct 'one first class of those functions.' He knew exactly what he wished to do but could not find a solution.

He went off on a geological excursion. 'The incidents of the travel,' said Poincaré, 'made me forget my mathematical work. Having reached Coutances, we entered an omnibus to go some place or other. At the moment when I put my foot on the step, the idea came to me, without anything in my former thoughts seeming to have paved the way for it, that the transformations I had used to define the Fuchsian functions were identical with those of non-Euclidian geometry. I did not verify the idea; I should not have had time, as, upon taking my seat in the omnibus, I went on with a conversation already commenced, but I felt a perfect certainty. On my return to Caen, for conscience' sake, I verified the result at my leisure.'

Next we may take up the testimony of an experimental physiologist, Walter B. Cannon [5]. 'The role of this unconscious work in mathematical invention,' says Poincaré, 'appears to me incontestable.' Cannon prefers the term *extraconscious* to *unconscious*. 'The operation going on in an industry under the immediate supervision of the director is like the cerebral processes to which we pay attention; but meanwhile in other parts of the industrial plant important work is proceeding which the director at the moment does not see. Thus also with extraconscious processes.'

He cites the experience of Charles Darwin, who had for years been storing up a tremendous armory of facts with the feeling that they might all be discharged at some great target he could not yet conceive. Suddenly what Graham Wallas later called 'the illumination' came. 'I can remember the very spot in the road,' Darwin wrote, 'whilst in my carriage, when to my joy, the solution occurred to me.' It was, of course, the theory of biological evolution.

Mentioning many cases in biological research and the like, Cannon refers to this end product of the imaginative process as 'a hunch'—a term that reminds us how common the phenomenon is to all of us. 'In typical cases,' he writes, 'a hunch appears after long study and springs into consciousness at a time when the investigator is not working on his problem. It arises from a wide knowledge of facts, but it is essentially a leap of the imagination, for it reaches forth into the range of possibilities. It results from a spontaneous process of creative thought.'

He cites his own famous discovery of 'the significance of bodily changes which occur in great emotional excitement.' Such changes 'seemed unrelated. Then, one wakeful night, after a considerable collection of these changes had been disclosed, the idea flashed through my mind that they could be nicely integrated if conceived as bodily preparations for supreme effort in flight or in fighting. Further investigation added to the collection and confirmed the general scheme suggested by the hunch.'

We may quote one more example, this time from the psychoanalyst Theodor Reik. [37] 'There are phases during analysis in which we arrive at psychological conclusions by means of reasoning. There are certain problems that can be solved by common sense and logic, it is true, but they are not the most important problems that face the psychoanalyst. He arrives at his deepest insights neither by searching for a conclusion nor by jumping to one. The best way is for him to wait until a conclusion jumps to him. It is at this moment when a longer or shorter suspense is lifted, when he has this special and psychologically significant, "Oh, that's it!"—experience.'

The syntax is doubtful but the sense clear. In these and scores of other cases, from almost as many fields, it is hard to escape the presumption that a common process is at work. Galton [15], Whitehead, Jaensch, Spearman, Koestler [29] and Read [36] have all hinted at it, in one way or another. Indeed, an elementary version of it may be found in the college textbooks on psychology. But what is nowhere, apparently, fully stated (so strong is the prestige of traditional 'deductive reasoning') is that this process, comprising and subordinating other methods, may in fact be the *major* mode of creative activity in every field, the 'natural' shorthand of the intelligence.

Let us try to define the steps of this imaginative series, in what appear to be their unchangeably consecutive order. Some of these steps may be jumped on occasion (Piaget notes this as a characteristic mental trait of children), though always at the risk of compromising the solution. We may suggest these:

(A) *The Hint.* Depending on the nature of the project, this may be of any species—a theme in music, a tentative hypothesis in physics, a problem in aeronautics, a phrase suggesting a poem. Or it may be a borrowing from one species to another—from biology to mathematics, for example, as Hermite [21] suggested. This last, like other hints, is perhaps an imaginative act in itself. In any case, almost at once the hint will begin to develop into a nebula that suggests the projected whole. The remarks of Mozart and Valéry are very enlightening on this point [21].

(B) *The Saturation.* If this stage seems to call for a basic distinction between the experience of artists and others, it is only because the psychic materials of the poet [30], the composer and the painter are largely already present in solution. This is the medium in which artists have their professional being, though they too must often make their more subtle kinds of research. But the novelist—an artist too, if he can earn that title—and perhaps a good many workers in other fields, must saturate themselves in the materials related to their subject. There is a good deal of disagreement on this point, chiefly as to the kind and degree of saturation required. It may be that this is governed by the types of data involved, or the field in which they are to be applied; or that the proportion of materials already present is the chief determinant. It is possible, too, that workers who object to documentation at this stage may have found that only materials which have gone

through the whole digestive cycle of the imagination are capable of forming the new combinations
they seek. Moreover, it may be that this digestive
cycle works at a different rate for each person. In
any event, saturation of some kind would appear
to be essential. *The imaginative process does not
produce something out of nothing. It produces
something out of something else.*

(c) *The Conscious Attack.* When these materials have been ingested, or even while they are
being assembled, the inquirer will make bold and
repeated attacks on his subject, testing it from
every quarter, and bringing all his conscious resources to bear on it. In many cases, even when
he is not engaged on a joint project, he will enlist
the suggestions of his colleagues—what the psychologists call *social facilitation* and the sociol-
ogists *social interaction.* (This is perhaps not ad-
visable for novelists or other artists, who may be
put off by any 'violation of privacy' in the imaginative process.) But such conscious attacks are
essential too. They open up lines of advance; and
the solution finally broached may be an 'impossible' combination of two or more of these lines,
bent into a single triumphant curve.

(d) *The Release.* This is the point at which the
inquirer, having done everything he can with
his subject in the way of conscious resourceful-
ness, simply drops it for a while. He drops it

completely, puts it 'out of his mind.' (This is, of course, just the opposite of what happens. Actually, he puts it *into* his mind.) He does this in perfect confidence that his work will not be lost. He simply *lets go*. Sartre [42] writes that 'the act of imagination is a magical one. It is an incantation destined to produce the object of one's thought, the thing one desires in a manner that one can take possession of it.' This is a fancifully accurate description, though it confuses one of the historical uses of the imaginative process, magic, with the thing itself. But the main point here is that the inquirer should let go. William James warns that the process may 'be actually interfered with (*jammed* as it were) by his voluntary efforts. . . .' The inquirer turns to something else—a trip, a party, a football game, a hobby, even some kind of work not involved with his project. The peculiarly lucid hallucination of a hangover is an especially favorable state. The poet Rimbaud, who was not so mad as he had been painted, spoke of the necessary condition, in a larger sense, as '*un long, immense et raissonné deréglèment de tout les sens.*' [43]

(E) *The Hidden Phase.* Graham Wallas calls this 'the germination.' Psychologists have attempted to explain what goes on during this phase in various terms: the unconscious, the extraconscious, hypothetical switching operations in the cortex, processes analogous to cybernetics, and so on.

Freud was more pessimistic. 'Unfortunately,' he wrote, 'before the problem of the creative artist, analysis must lay down its arms.' This question as to the precise nature of the creative act is, perhaps, the core problem of the artist, or any investigator. We do not understand what happens; but there is no reason to suppose that we may not find out. All we know is that certain procedures — often, but by no means invariably — will lead us to certain results. There is a kind of absent-minded conspiracy to obscure this fact. An engineer does not like to acknowledge that he does not *know* how he arrived at his solution. It seems less than intellectually respectable — or worse yet, downright impractical and risky — to be solving problems by means we do not comprehend. But the test, of course, lies in the results.

(F) *The Illumination.* The exclamation of Archimedes is obviously the right word for that moment of sudden illumination which reveals the key to the whole — just as the experience of Archimedes is perhaps our first familiar instance of the process itself. Koestler uses the same example. Both Reik and Whitehead mention 'the state of imaginative muddled suspense' [49] which precedes this *ecce signum;* and almost every observer reports the startled joy with which it is greeted. It is *recognized*, at once, as the desired answer. This recognition may suggest some earlier and not quite realized precognition. What is far more likely, however, is that the preliminary conscious work has defined the contours of the country and sketched a network of possible trails through it. Then the moment of illumination picks out the one best route and brings it suddenly into focus.

(G) *The Verification.* The question to be asked of any such discovery is, of course: Will it work? It should be tested by every means at hand, until the chance of error has been brought down to a minimum. Even at this stage, one of the earlier solutions need not be entirely ruled out. It may be reconsidered as a check, or even as a possible alternative. But it should not be favored, out of mere caution, as against the more daring but also more satisfactory imaginative concept. In some fields, of course, this would be impossible. There is only one answer. In others, there may be a choice, and thus some danger that the startling quality of the imaginative solution may react against it.

Perhaps it needs to be pointed out again that the function we have described is only one of many historically assigned to the imagination. Its reliance on the manifold aspects of perception is clear, though not exclusive. Other factors are involved. Rationalists, if there are any left, will not like it. Though scientists use it, it is not perhaps 'scientific,' and will not be until physiologists, neurologists and psychologists can tell us more about its behavior. But it *is* good, sound instrumentalism. By and large, it works.

From Philostratus down, the history of 'imagination' is a strange business. It has been confused with purely intellectual invention (which, as we have seen, may not be so 'pure' as we had supposed); with fancy, fantasy, and with plain day or night dreaming. It has been paired with such psychologically disreputable sisters as 'intuition.' It has, over long periods, been ceded to the estheticians, and thus subtly discredited among 'practical' men, while at the same time it was being developed as a matter *peculiar* to the arts. By the same token, certain materials—so-called 'images' or 'percepts'— were exclusively identified with it, thus confusing the material with the process, and ruling out other types of materials.

In Part Two we shall see how the imaginative series can be adapted to the preparation of a novel. The novel is an extremely complex case: the variety of materials, the major imaginative act that conceives 'the sense of the whole,' and the thousands of minor interwoven acts.

The analogy with Mozart's account of his conception of a piece of music is beautifully suggestive. 'Once I have my theme, another melody comes, linking itself to the first one, in accordance with the needs of the composition as a whole . . . The work grows; I keep expanding it, conceiving it more and more clearly until I have the entire composition finished in my head though it may be long. . . . It does not come to me successively, with its various parts worked out in detail, as they will be later on, but it is in its entirety that my imagination lets me hear it. . . .' [21]

11 time: tense: duration: pace: simultaneity

Among other things, the novel is a progression in both actual and imaginary time—actual in the writing or reading, imaginary in the events of the story itself.

Its time relations are many, complex and interactive.

The chief external time factors are writing time—for the whole book, or any part—and reading time. In their effects, at least, these are not so obvious as they may appear.

The time factors in the book itself, however, will be much more various and intimately related. (A) The period in which the book is set—the 1880s, the 1980s, or some quite nebulous or imaginary era. (B) The duration, or duration series, of the action. Duration: 1880–1882. Duration series: 1920–1925;

1933–1939; 1941–1945. (c) The tense or tenses in which the action is treated—past, perfect, historical present, etc., or any combination of these. (d) The over-all pace of a novel—deliberate, brisk, very rapid—and the minor variations of pace within this dominant. (e) Simultaneous narratives—that is, two or more overt stories, separate (Faulkner: *The Wild Palms*), or intercut and interwoven (*Men of Good Will*), but all conforming to the major time scheme of the novel. (f) Simultaneous treatment— an attempt to render the concurrent unfolding phases of an event more or less as they occur (Conrad: *The Shadow Line;* Ralph Bates: *Rainbow Fish*). (g) Elastic time—a foreshortening or drawing out, according to the fullness of treatment required for each section. (h) Deployable time—a time scheme that makes use of so-called flashbacks, future scenes out of regular order, and a movement back and forth in the progression of the main narrative. This is closely related to, but not identical with, (i) narrator's time. Here the narrator, like Conrad's Marlow in *Lord Jim,* may establish his own scene-and-time convention for the act of story-telling, and employ still another for the story itself. Or he may recount the story entirely in the past. Or he may "act out" the story, as it were, simultaneously with the other characters. (j) Subjective time—that is, the time flow of a character's conscious or unconscious mind, as distinguished from the time of the external events through which he is moving. (k) Multiple time levels. A novel will often have more than one level of meaning (the explicit, the socially typical, the symbolic, etc.), and each level may call for its appropriate, though perhaps only slightly variant, time scheme.

Two or more of these time conventions, plus others not mentioned here, may be symbiotic in a particular novel.

How long will it take to write the book? This is one of the more incalculable things about any novel, and should be treated as such. Even if they make very large allowances, the writer who promises a book on a certain date and the publisher who believes him are acting in blind faith. (They are both usually well aware of this.) The testimony of some very skilful and industrious novelists appears to show that, if the book is to be as good as the writer can make it, he will nearly always spend more time than he intended on it. Many kinds of miscalculation can be discounted in advance. But a stubborn passage may hold out for days against his best attack; or he may discover new and valid growth lines. Even Thomas Mann, a superb technician, began *Death in Venice* with the idea of doing a neat short story.

Writing speed has certain definite effects on the quality of a book. Every novelist will have his own "normal" writing speed, the pace natural to him when things are going well. But at first, he may have some trouble finding this. If he works too slowly, the rhythmic effect of the book is likely to be weak, or halting, or stiff. If he drives hard, the charge of energy expanded may get into the work as (A) eloquence, or (B) nervous urgency. The latter is a quality particularly admired by American novelists and readers. The disadvantages of the method are that it enforces shortcuts and simplifications, and that—like American life in general—it sacrifices feeling tone to sensational values.

The reading time is, or should be, under the persuasive control of the novelist. He has a hundred means at hand to suggest the tempo of the long, easy passage, like a ship running large; or of nervous action lighted by violence; or of the quiet flames in a hearth.

The explicit duration of the action in a novel may theoretically be one minute or thousands of years. This raises questions of relativity we are not equipped to solve. The term *duration series* is intended to indicate those segments of time comprised in the parts of a novel—typically, a chronicle novel—separated by gaps, but arranged consecutively. The events taking place in such gaps may, of course, be dealt with elsewhere in the novel.

The choice of a tense or tenses is not difficult, except in novels having an especially intricate time scheme. There the simplest is often the best. Any system of overlapping tenses may involve the writer in difficulties beyond his control—and well beyond the reader's patience.

In general, the past tense is usual. The historical present may be effective in the display of sharp action or hallucinatory states; but it tends to seem obtrusive or artificial after a few pages, especially if it is used as a dominant tense.

The over-all pace of a novel is a major choice, like the choice of subject or viewpoint. Perhaps the only large miscalculation evident in the work of Henry James is that he neglected to suit his pace to the particular demands of each subject. This is somewhat less true of the earlier books than of the later ones.

Even more than the other factors in a novel, viewpoint, subject and pace are all closely interlocked. If the most promising narrator for a subject has been chosen, the fact that this narrator has a quick, edgy mind may in itself dictate a nervous pace; and this nervous pace may be precisely what is needed to furnish the sense of incidental movement for a subject that is somewhat deliberate in its unfolding. Or the reverse may be true, for other reasons. Each novel is a particular problem.

The minor variations of pace, within the dominant tempo and subordinate to it, will have their effect

largely in terms of what Kenneth Burke calls 'qualitative progression' [3]—a stretch of hard action
making us desire a leisurely interval, or the calm
rhythm of a sailor's life at sea preparing us for the
excitement of landing in a big city. Elastic time—
a foreshortening or drawing out of actual time—is,
of course, a function of the narrative method. We
may note here that the novelist can 'make time
stand still,' as Proust does, while he probes at the
core of each consciousness in an event; or he may
rush us along so rapidly that the detail blurs like
a fast pan shot in a motion picture. The resource-
ful novelist is seldom bound by chronographic time.
He *is* obliged to adhere to, and to make us believe
in, the time dimension he has set.

The varieties of novelist's time we have discussed
so far have all been time-in-line, a more or less
continuous forward movement from one point to
another—what is called *straight narrative*.

There are other varieties. One of these is deployable time, which resembles a kind of purposeful
play with a deck of cards. The value of the whole
deck remains constant, but the cards may be arranged in any order or combination for any desired
result.

The limitations on deployable time are stringent: it
should be made use of only when the required effects can be gained in no other way. Observant

readers will note how seldom, relatively speaking, James found it necessary. Its inherent dangers are overelaboration and artificiality—both miscalculations of means. The reader may be wearied into confusion by a constant crisscross in the time convention. There is a chance too—it happened, to some extent, in at least one of Conrad's novels, *Nostromo*—that the shuffling of time values may cancel out as a virtual stasis in the major movement of the story.

One aspect in which narrator's time differs from deployable time is that it appears to be, not a more or less arbitrary arrangement by the author, but a function of the narrator's perception, reflection or memory. It happens in a defined human consciousness; and in ordinary social give-and-take we are so accustomed to casual associations, memories called up by an apparently irrelevant remark, and other such matters that, rightly persuaded, we will accept even a very complicated time scheme as "natural" to the narrator's personality. We say that it is 'just the way his mind works.'

Subjective time is, in one sense, the 'pure' form of deployable time and narrator's time. But in the sense in which we use it here it becomes a counterpoint to the overt narrative; and its particular values as incidence and commentary are best brought out in that way. The danger in subjective time is that it may operate as 'psychology for its own sake'—the documentation or analysis of a mind as information rather than as narrative process. [3]

Necessarily we tend more and more to think of time in terms of concomitant space. We say casually: 'It's an hour by plane from New York to Washington.' But it was a good deal longer, and thus farther perhaps, when Washington himself traveled the distance by coach.

The novelist must be constantly aware of the fact that our time sense, in life or in the novel, seldom corresponds to the measurement of the clock. Our hearts speed up and quicken time, or slow down and make it drag. And the clock is arbitrary, not our hearts. A man who has been hanging over a cliff will say: 'It seemed like a hundred years.' But a girl who has had a good time at a dance exclaims: 'It was over before I knew it.'

12 process

We have been using the word *process* in the standard dictionary meanings. Now—alas for exact terminology—we must employ it in a strict and exclusive technical sense.

We may say that *process* comprises, with distinctions, the older meanings of *composition, form* and *plot*. It is the principle of conversion by means of which the subject may be projected in the shape of the reader's interest and presumptive wishes or fears, but on the writer's terms. (When the terms are also, presumably, the reader's, the book may be regarded as "popular" literature. The distinction, however, is relative.) It seems better to substitute *process* for *composition* or *form*. *Composition*, as applied to writing, has the uncomfortable connotation of a writing exercise. As Herbert Read says, we do 'form' things [36]; but in general *form* suggests a mold, something fixed, an order-by-fiat—all notions foreign to the active time-flow of *process* in literature. *Plot* is, in fact, a kind of order-by-intellectual-fiat, and may be described as petrified process.

Like viewpoint, process is a principle of selection and a way of handling things. It is the conveyor of symbols in their growth and themes in their unfolding. It helps to project and control key and scale and duration and character. It is even, in Burke's sense, 'style'—that is, 'minor form'—so that a trope in the sentence becomes, as it were, the equivalent of a symbol in the whole book. But chiefly, perhaps, it is the major means of organizing coherence in a novel, 'the sense of the whole' in operative terms.

In our meaning, process becomes a multiplicity and variety of implicit promises made to the reader—promises that certain things may happen to people he is interested in: the characters. These promises, like many of those in our own lives, are usually provisional. They will be made good, or canceled, or turned into their opposites, or renewed in another guise. They may be short-term promises, which lead into still others; or long-term promises, which conduct us to the terminal or solution of the book itself—usually a climax.

Two points should be firmly stressed. (A) All process is by definition a *vehicle*. It *carries* something else—anything and everything, from the major sense of the book to the tinting of some casual episode. Even in the barest melodrama, process should never be explicit. If it is, we smile and say that 'the plot shows.' The only exception, perhaps, is 'conventional form,' in which we expect certain procedures and are aware that we expect them. But even in this case, the awareness is a function of ritual expectancy, which is in turn one aspect of the repeatedly familiar. If we had not seen 'conventional form' so often before—in the novel, that is— we should not know how to demand 'conventionality' of it.

(B) By the same token, every pattern of process is capable of a variety of uses. The same vehicle may, at different times, carry its metaphorical freight of joy or anger, a twinkling spring day or a ship in trouble at sea, the unfolding character of an ambitious man or a dreaming child.

Here and in other places, we are so much indebted to Kenneth Burke's formulations that we should be

less than generous if we accorded him the doubtful
honor of a collaborator's part. Readers who first
came upon his work in the *Dial* and other magazines of the 1920s, especially the pieces later collected in *Counter-Statement,* will remember the
concentrated shock of enlightenment in that discovery. It is not too much to say that some of us
'learned our business,' in large part, from him. Since
then he has reached out into the whole field of lan-
guage as 'symbolic action.' But even if we had no
evidence beyond that first book of definitions, we
might still, after twenty-five years, regard him as
perhaps the most important theoretical critic of
literature so far in the twentieth century.

One discovery alone—laid down simply enough,
and never, so far as we know, fully developed—
might have earned him that judgment. 'There are
formal patterns,' Burke writes, 'which distinguish
our experience. They apply in art, since they apply
outside of art. The accelerated motion of a falling
body, the cycle of a storm, the gradations of a sun-
rise, the stages of a cholera epidemic, the ripening
of crops—in all such instances we find the material
of progressive form. Repetitive form applies to all
manner of orientation, for we can continue to dis-
cuss a subject only by taking up in turn various
aspects of it. . . . Thus, though forms need not be
prior to experience, they are certainly prior to the
work of art exemplifying them. Psychology and
philosophy may decide whether they are innate or

resultant; so far as the work of art is concerned they simply *are:* when one turns to the production or enjoyment of a work of art, a formal equipment is already present, and the effects of art are involved in its utilization.'

This has so many fruitful aspects that we do not know where to take hold of it first. But we recognize its quality at once. It is an 'illumination' of the first order. At one stroke it undercuts the historical notions of form as ritual, form as logical order, form as a 'classical' requirement, form as the uninterrupted flow of 'romantic' inspiration (which is often the absence of, or revolt from, *any* effective process), form as traditional authority, and so on. It allows us to recognize these notions as what they are—power devices, intended to twist literature to other uses, social or factional or personal. But it does not deny the valid elements of process in such forms, mistaken as their program may be.

It does these, and other things, by showing us *where the process begins*—the immemorial roots that produce the infinitely various flowers. And in doing this, it gives the novelist, or any artist, an unassailable mode of operation. It needs no defense, no authority, no sanction, no rationalization, no 'esthetic' equipment that differs in *kind* from the equipment of everyone. (We may note here, almost incidentally, the profound effect of democratization in such a principle.) Out of the patterns we make in living, like the remembered line of flight a swallow traces across the sky at dusk, we derive a procedure that serves equally well to chart the long veerings of a woman's love, the ups and downs of a business career, or the agitation in the mind of a frightened child.

Moreover, this derivation of process, as Burke notes, offers us at once a principle of projection for the writer and a principle of reception for the reader. They are the same principle, and it is universal, in varying degrees and configurations. Thus Burke can make 'form' (process) synonymous with 'psychology' ('the psychology of the audience'), and both with 'eloquence,' which he defines as 'the end of art, and thus its essence'—the full, rich and various realization of many orders of process in the intense 'individuation' of a work of art.

We note, indeed, that the principle may be carried far beyond Burke's original formulation. It opens out the horizon like a climbing plane. Nor would it be rash to suggest that this concept promises a proliferation of 'forms' limited only by the analytic imagination of the writer. We have seen that it derives from all the orders of human experience—the sensational, the motor, the kinesthetic, the 'intuitive,' the perceptual, the imaginative, the conceptual, the emotional, and so on. From each of these it draws recurrent patterns which may become the common currency of process in literature.

Plainly we may find as many kinds of process available to the novel—or to poetry, or music, or drama—as there are recognizable patterns in human experience; and it is clear that we have hardly begun to explore these patterns as yet. Except in the case of rhythm, perhaps, we are familiar only with a few of the grosser ones, grossly analyzed. We have 'lived' many of the others; we have not yet realized them. Thus, out of the tremendous variety of psychophysical patterns made available in a constantly expanding human experience, we may be confident that we shall be able to derive a plenitude of new or variant processes applicable to literature.

We have been hoarding what appears to be a serious objection. If *all* the patterns of experience, even freshly discovered ones, are theoretically to be employed as process in literature, how can we hope that the reader will recognize them? The answer, of course, is that we cannot, except perhaps in the wistful and quizzical way that Henry James expressed such a hope in *The Pattern in the Carpet*. The reader does not *need* to be conscious of them in order to feel their effect.

We must repeat our earlier warning here. Any device of process is a *vehicle*. It has no content. It is not capable of producing an effect in itself—even in music. It is the *carrier* of a theme, a symbol, 'the sense of the whole.' There is danger of confusion here, especially in regard to the great classic themes —death and rebirth, the journey, the return—which have by their very nature taken on something of the character of formal patterns. They are still, by our definition, *themes,* not *process.*

We may demonstrate this in a simple transvaluation. Let us substitute for Odysseus, the Ithacan hero, the personality of Maui, the Polynesian trickster hero, who is also returning home by sea from a war. Then let us transpose the adventurous-heroic key of the *Odyssey* into the comic-heroic key of the Maui legends. Obviously, even if we employ much the same formal devices, they will carry quite different materials and be aimed at dissimilar effects. We have a further example, of course, in Joyce's *Ulysses.*

It may be that there is a morphology of process in the novel—a theory that gives us a convenient handle on such terms as *ritual, plot* and Burke's *conventional form.* We may suggest that the novel, and perhaps all literature, display two major types of process: *ritual process* and *autogenous process.* (We do not mean to set up a dualism. It just happens that there seem to be two.)

The first, ritual process, imposes an exterior sanction or authority of some kind, antecedent to the work. We may cite Jane Harrison's description of the prescribed forms in Greek drama [22]; Saints-

bury's remarks on the poetry contests of Toulouse
[40]; English and French classicist literature of the
eighteenth century; French Symbolist poetry; the
commercial Broadway play; and the plot story of
the American magazines.

Among these odd bedfellows we find little in common but the fact that they are all submitted to an
a priori mandate of some kind—religious, traditional, didactic, commercial, or merely programmatic. Each work must conform to specifications. It
must fit a mold. If it does so, it is eligible to share
the prestige of the molding agent. From this we
may deduce the authority of 'plot' as an antecedent
and semi-independent factor to which the individual work must adapt itself, whether we are concerned with the 'plot' of a drama by Sophocles or
the 'plot' of an American popular novel. The line of
descent appears to be more or less direct, the prestige element somewhat comparable, and the factor
of an external agent compromising the autonomy
of the work virtually identical. We may surmise
that the hallowed villain of the piece is plainly to
be found in Aristotle's *Poetics*.

The second type, autogenous process, answers in
general to Burke's description of 'form.' It com-
mands no external sanction or authority, except for
a certain measure of usage and its origins in those
psychophysical patterns which supply a code of signals between novelist and reader. But even these

are not in any sense prescriptive. They are not even rules of thumb. They are simply the equipment we bring to all living. The novelist selects among them, according to his needs, and brings them into a highly organized relationship with each other, a relationship largely determined by the nature and interaction of the materials they have been chosen to convey.

We have all seen actual living situations in which the movement of people and events is so formally 'right' that someone is sure to remark: 'It's just like a story.' Anyone who has ever been in love will recall something like that feeling, especially in the early stages: the heightened sensitivity to circumstances and events, their effect of almost mystical significance, and what seems to be the inevitable 'rightness' of the procedures—whether things are going well or ill. But there is also sometimes a sense of fatedness not usually present in a good novel.

In general, however, the analogy holds. Autogenous process in the novel does resemble those life experiences intensified and made coherent by some organizing situation or emotion; and our feeling that they are 'like a story' displays our recognition of the psychophysical patterns common to life experience and to the novel. The key word is 'organizing.' In both cases, it is the heightened intensity derived from organization that produces the recognition and the effect.

But the chief point to be made about autogenous process is that it must be an organization within the work, in terms of the work, and largely determined by the work. We might bring it to a *reductio ad absurdum* and say that the work must be allowed to organize itself. In any case, if we can assert any antecedent principle as inviolable, it is that the autonomy of the particular work must be dominant. It is as nearly an absolute as anything can be in literature. It is the controlling principle, not only in terms of autogenous process, but of the whole organization of the work.

Our adventitious dualism show signs of becoming a dichotomy, and we must proceed to break it down a little. (For once we may make a flat statement, on that most tentative of subjects, the genetics of literature, in which every general proposition is eternally compromised by the fact that it does not derive from or refer to a particular case. We should like to maintain that *all* cases in literature are particular cases, except that (A) this too would be a general proposition, and (B) it would logically enjoin us to stop there.)

The statement we set out to make is that nearly all literary process is mixed in character, derivation and history. Thus our dualism is to some extent arbitrary. Kenneth Burke's category of 'conventional form' provides us with an excellent laboratory specimen. '. . . when a form appeals as form,' he writes, 'we designate it as conventional form. Any form can become conventional, and be sought for itself . . . We might note, in conventional form, the element of "categorical expectancy." That is, whereas the anticipations and gratifications of progressive and repetitive form arise *during the process* of reading, the expectations of conventional form may be *anterior to* the reading.'

Thus, at first glance, 'conventional form' would appear to be identical with our ritual process. But we do not need Burke's warning that this subject 'has brought out the extremes of aesthetic acuity and aesthetic bluntness' to be reminded that the elements in 'conventional form' are far more mixed than that. Without going over most of the ground Burke has covered so well, we may mention and extend a few points. He notes the 'categorical expectancy' of a beginning as a beginning, an ending as an ending, etc. These may be ritual process, as in the prologue and epilogue of a Restoration comedy. But are they not also autogenous process, since they derive from the psychophysical expectancies of birth and death, the rising and setting of the sun, the first of the year and the end of the year?

This brings us to a dilemma. Clearly, now, *both* ritual process and autogenous process ultimately spring from the psychophysical patterns common to human experience. But in every case, ritual process involves the intervention of the *group* at some point, under religious, traditional, critical or other sanctions. The purpose of this intervention is conservative. It is intended to fix a particular association of process, plus concomitant themes and other elements, and to insure their repetition. It demands repetition-with-variation; and is not repetition-with-variation precisely one of the types of autogenous form?

Thus, if the analogy is not too far-fetched, it may be that a convention or school of the novel repeats, in the large, one of the interior aspects of process in the novel itself. Moreover, since all literature is a tradition, even the most original uses of autogenous process will be influenced to some extent by former uses, modes and traditions. 'Categorical expectancy' is never wholly absent, even though it may be served only by giving us the opposite of what we had expected. Perhaps we may conclude that our two orders of process, the ritual and the autogenous, are strong directional emphases rather than mutually exclusive types.

We may infer a typical morphology in the conventions and processes of the novel. In any well-developed literary period, there will be a few novelists of the highest talent, a more numerous group of those in the second class, a still larger number of third-class talents, and so on—in short, a kind of hierarchy, broadest at the base. We are concerned here with their genuine merits, which may or may not correspond to the estimates of their contemporaries. In any case, all these levels of talent are necessary to the full cultivation of such a period. Working together, and aware of each other, they create the germinal thickness and complexity of the literary medium.

In a period of this kind, some writer of the first talent will discover a fresh application of process in the novel. He will do this as the specific solution to a particular problem, and pass on to something else. A few writers of the second order will adapt this, in limited ways, to their still highly original work. Novelists of the third class, borrowing from the second, will generalize it; and thus an aspect of process will be passed down the line until even the editors of pulp magazines begin to question its overfamiliarity. It degenerates, in successive stages, from discovery to a limited adaptation, a generalization, a plot device, a trick and a cliché. It may go out of use entirely, or be revamped for other purposes, or lie dormant for a while until it is taken up again.

We have an excellent example in the so-called stream-of-consciousness device—in its origins, at least, a bastardization of the documentary interior monologue and the genuine imaginative dramatization of personality. Credited to an earlier French novelist, Dujardin, of the late nineteenth century, it may be said to have appeared as a kind of highly

rationalized soliloquy in the work of Marcel Proust.
By the 1930s, it had shown its full power in *Ulysses*,
turned to running quicksilver in the novels of Virginia Woolf, and been put to various uses by Dorothy Richardson, Waldo Frank, William Faulkner
and others. Thereafter shoals of minor novelists
took it up. Long before the middle of the century, it
was established as respectable tender in the American popular magazine, and its subsequent career
might easily be predicted. The progressive steriliza-
tion of the materials it carried, from *Ulysses* to the
Saturday Evening Post, is not our topic here. We
need only observe that this censorship-by-gentle-
man's-agreement had ironically destroyed its sole
usefulness as a device for revealing the private—
and thus by its very definition 'improper'—mind-
stream of a character. It had been reduced to a
meaningless rhetorical trick.

13 modes of process

Burke [3] mentions five aspects of 'form,' the first
two subsumed under the head of 'progressive form.'
They are:

(A) 'Syllogistic progression,' which he defines as
'the form of a perfectly conducted argument, ad-
vancing step by step. It is the form of a mystery
story . . .'

(B) 'Qualitative progression . . . Instead of one
incident in the plot preparing us for some other pos-

sible incident of plot (as Macbeth's murder of
Duncan prepares us for the dying of Macbeth), the
presence of one quality prepares us for the introduction of another (the grotesque seriousness of
the murder scene preparing us for the grotesque
buffoonery of the porter scene).'

(c) 'Repetitive form is the consistent maintaining
of a principle under new guises. . . . It is our only
method of "talking on the subject." '

(d) 'Conventional form . . . the appeal of form as
form.'

(e) 'Minor or incidental forms. . . . Their effect
partially depends upon their function in the whole,
yet they manifest sufficient evidences of episodic
distinctness to bear consideration apart from their
context.'

Burke develops these aspects of form with a persuasive thoroughness we cannot hope to match here.
He points out that there may be an interrelation of
processes—one type is seldom found alone—or a
conflict of processes, inadvertent or planned.

It is necessary to note that his definition of 'syllogistic progression' as a 'perfectly conducted argument'
is evidently metaphorical. We may infer that he
means, not formal logic, but strict human logic—
that is, what we feel *must* happen in the given cir-

cumstances. 'Qualitative progression' is, of course, our old friend 'contrast,' but contrast given a new cogency in terms of our organic expectations. Not *any* contrast will do. It should be one of those kinds of 'qualitative progression' we are conditioned to anticipate in stress and release, the swell before a storm at sea, rest after labor, coming out of the dark into a lighted room, and so on. (The examples are ours, but typically Burkesque.)

We may offer a few more examples. 'Conventional form': a baseball crowd stands up at the outset of the seventh inning. But this is also, perhaps, and originally, 'qualitative progression': after six innings the muscles need stretching. 'Repetitive form': the comic discrepancy between Mr. Pickwick's reputed wisdom and his inability to cope with each new situation.

'Syllogistic progression': Gustave shoots Honoré and robs him, after having first shot Honoré's friend Prosper. Or a single reversal: Gustave shoots Honoré and robs him. Prosper, who is Honoré's friend, shoots Gustave. Or a double peripeteia: Gustave tries to rob Honoré, but Honoré shoots him. Prosper, mistaking Honoré for Gustave, shoots Honoré. These devices have been in use since Aristotle and have long since descended the Avernal levels from process to cliché. The predominant use of 'syllogistic progression,' in fact, is a mark of the 'plotting' novelist. A more legitimate example of reversal may be found in Catherine's final rejection of Morris Townsend in *Washington Square* — though this too is compromised in the sense that it embodies James's typical rejection pattern.

'Minor form': 'The Town-Ho's Story' in *Moby Dick;* the Bossuet research in *Isabelle:* Madame Jupillon's affectionate dogs in *Germinie Lacerteux*. The first is a well-rounded example of minor process — perhaps almost too much of a story-in-itself, but functional in the major narrative — of a kind frequent in Shakespeare, where Melville probably learned its use. Vincent suggests, indeed, that this is the core of the first-version 'whaling story' out of which *Moby Dick* grew. [46] The Bossuet thesis in *Isabelle* serves as Lacase's introduction to the chateau at La Quartfourche, where the main story is set. But it is carried through the book to some extent, and thus becomes a major 'repetitive form.' In the Goncourts' novel, Madame Jupillon's dogs are very incidental 'minor form.' But in the sense that they show us one more aspect of Germinie's hunger for affection, they too are 'repetitive form.'

We may go beyond Burke and suggest one or two types of our own. The first is a restatement of his 'five aspects.'

(A) *Synergetic Process.* Burke mentions the crossing, recrossing and combination of the several aspects of process. We wish to point out that these crossings and combinations are most often salient at key points in a novel, notably the climax. It is clear that when two or more lines of process are drawn together in this way, the effect is usually greater than the sum of the parts, just as the contextual effect of a sentence is greater than the sum of the words that compose it. Plainly a further aspect of process is at work here, and that aspect can be nothing less than the functional 'sense of the whole.'

We may clarify the point by reversing it. If the individual lines of process did *not* touch or join, if they ran as mere parallels from beginning to end of the novel (a contingency we can hardly imagine), we should have nothing but implicit relations between them, set out in terms of a difficult simultaneity. We are forced to assume that synergetic process is one aspect, perhaps a major aspect, of constructive movement in the novel.

Only this type of process can weave the finely articulated net of such a novel as *The Ambassadors* or *The Magic Mountain,* in which all the possible combinations of elements, within the given compass, are virtually exhausted. Moreover, it is strikingly evident in such 'collective' novels as *U. S. A.* Here the predominance of the whole over any single part is necessarily so urgent that synergetic process tends to overshadow the other elements of 'form.' But the mutual reinforcement and intensification of effects to be derived from its combinative function is perhaps even more sharply picked out in such closely woven short novels as *The Aspern Papers* or *Mario and the Magician.*

We may define synergetic process as 'the sense of the whole' in operative terms. Nor does it violate our basic notion of 'form' as a promise. In literature, as in other kinds of life, the promise that things will come together is one of the most attractive and fruitful of promises. It is a basic mode of human living: the principle of combination and multiplication originally derived from the organic, in marriage and parenthood, but carried out in the social forms of the party, the dance, the club, the neighborhood, the commercial company, the political group, or any human society. More than that, it is germinative in itself. It leads into forever new combinations, as the child grows into new marriages and new children.

(B) *Disjunctive Process.* This might almost be defined as the opposite of 'syllogistic progression.' Hence we may say that, in one of its aspects, it resembles a mystery story without a solution. Thus it violates an older kind of 'categorical expectancy' in favor of a newer one. In general, we may describe it as progression by disconnected suggestion. Still somewhat rare in the novel, it is a commonplace of twentieth-century drama and music, developed in many modes from ballet and the expressionist play to Stravinsky and bebop jazz. In nearly all these cases it may be said to have reached a new 'conventional form.'

The unresolved incident; the progression suddenly broken off, or involved in dissonance with a second; the gratuitous event, not to be accounted for; the character revealing himself in unprepared and surprising turns of behavior, acceptable once they are known; the exfoliation of a trivial mystery that suggests the inexplicable mysteries of life itself; human involvements so numerous, rapid and indeterminate that they remind us of William James's 'big buzzing confusion' of consciousness:—all these are aspects of disjunctive process.

We may find many of them in the work of Chekhov, Virginia Woolf, Dos Passos, Jean Giraudoux, and others. In Graham Greene's novels, the materials are presented first as disjunctive process combined with the 'syllogistic progression' of a mystery story. They are resolved in a purely 'syllogistic' climax. Thus the reader is doubly reassured. He has been delivered from both 'rational' and 'irrational' mysteries by 'rational' means alone.

Perhaps only in such a novel as Henry Green's *Concluding* does the disjunctive process become programmatic and dominant throughout. The immediate effect is disconcerting. We are so used to climactic resolution in the novel that when we are let down, as it were, without it, we tend to feel baffled and cheated. This is, of course, a demand for 'conventional form.' But the whole procedure of *Concluding* is realized with such clean and delicate skill that we should be hesitant about asking anything more of it. Whatever we might ask would almost certainly not be germane to its intention and effect.

We need to point out that a novel in which disjunctive process is the dominant will inevitably call for the most exact and superlative handling. It is not relieved from the usual requirements of tone, balance, 'the sense of the whole,' and that unity-in-diversity of which Burke speaks. Its very discontinuances make all these factors more difficult to catch. But, like the other aspects of process we have mentioned, it has its roots deep in our psychophysical patterns—in the nervous, broken rhythms of the twentieth century.

Here we may add two fairly trustworthy rules of thumb.

(A) A predominance of long-term promises, combined with a lack of well-developed 'minor forms,' will cause the reader to skip. Its effect is to make him impatient to discover 'how things come out.'

(B) A predominance of shorter promises and 'minor forms,' coupled with an insufficiency of long lines, will cause the reader to focus too much of his interest on the immediate scene. This is a characteristic fault of short-story writers who invade the novel. Its effects may be seen in the kind of book the reader does not finish.

It is the business of the novelist to conduct events in such a way that the outcome is inseparable from the sequence.

14 themes

Themes are the long lines of the subject. The action flows along these long lines as the action of our days moves along the lines of habits, requirements, expectancies, customs and affections. Like these living ways, themes may be diverted, reversed, combined with others, set at cross purposes, even suddenly broken off. They are the principles of continuity in a subject. They resemble cables, psychological drives, the movement toward a goal, a ship's voyage from her port of departure to her port of destination.

Themes are not process, though they resemble process perhaps more than any other element in the novel, and are frequently confused with it. They are materials which must be conveyed by devices of process. The distinction is basic. A theme, at least in the terms of its presentation, is indigenous to a particular novel. A device of process may be put to a variety of uses in any novel.

We may note the qualifying phrase: 'at least in the terms of its presentation.' This is necessary because a device of process and a specific kind of theme may *both* derive from our psychophysical or social patterns of experience. Certain themes of this type *have* been adapted over and over to new uses. That is, a pattern of meaning and its constituent vehicle of process have been transposed, more or less modified, from one context to another. We may observe this procedure at its barest in the so-called 'switch' that makes a new joke out of an old one. But this does not compromise our distinction between theme and process.

We may pick out two main types of theme. These are the *theme as aura*—in the sense of 'a subtle emanation proceeding from a body and surrounding it as an atmosphere'—and the *theme as ligament*.

The sense of fate in certain novels by Thomas Hardy provides us with a good example of the aural theme. Here the thematic content is so interfused with the whole body of the material that it becomes a property, an emanation, of the whole. The effect of a willing eagerness for experience in Conrad's *Youth* is a like case. This air of being a property of the whole, plus its conceptual quality, is what distinguishes an aural theme from atmosphere per se, though atmosphere, like tone, key and other elements, may contribute to the effect. We should observe, in both examples, that other types of themes are present and help to reinforce the aural theme.

The theme as ligament may be noted in the rather obvious progression of the major symbol in *The Scarlet Letter;* in the subtle growth of the parson's love for the blind girl in *The Pastoral Symphony;* or in the stylized repetitive pattern of Teague's ambition for politics, women, business, the law, and so on, in Brackenridge's *Modern Chivalry*—a pattern more or less duplicated, oddly enough, in *Bouvard and Pécuchet.* This, in its many variations, is the familiar 'long line' that draws the reader forward from the outset to the goal.

We may divide the major types into three suborders of themes:

(A) Certain themes will occur to the novelist as 'ideas.' These must be translated into the experiential series of his action and characters. Thus, if a novelist wishes to represent the 'futility' of human effort, he may show us a furious man beating against the circumstances of his life until he is finally broken by them.

(B) Another type of theme is Burke's 'verbal parallel to a pattern of experience.' He takes as an example the story of the King and the Peasant, and shows how it may be 're-individuated' as 'The Man Against the Mob, or A Saint Dying in Neglect.' This is our meaning-plus-process above, adaptable to a variety of contexts. It may also be the development line of a symbol.

(c) Other themes may be evolved out of the emerging order of the material. The revealing of character may be itself thematic; or the progress of a business speculation; or the onset and culmination of a love affair. All these display that promise, development, thwarting, variation, new promise and fulfillment which may show the line of a theme. And all these may be arranged to carry a series of intimations larger than the action itself.

15 symbols

'A study of symbolism is annoying, we must admit,' Burke writes, 'because it requires us continually to be "off the subject." If a writer speaks of life on a mountain, for instance, we start with the impertinent question, "What is he talking about?" We automatically assume that he is *not* talking about life on a mountain (not talking *only* about that).' [4]

Burke defines the symbol as 'the verbal parallel to a pattern of experience.' In general, we have chosen to include this sense among the several meanings of the term *theme*, and to confine *symbol* to its more familiar definitions as a token, a sign, 'something used or regarded as standing for or representing something else.' [1B] Thus, in Fitzgerald's *The*

Great Gatsby, the green light on the pier would be, in itself, a rather literal symbol—of Gatsby's romantic devotion, of his 'extraordinary gift for hope.' The associations are obvious: green as the color of hope, the green light as a go-ahead signal in traffic, etc. But insofar as it is used in a consecutive system of references, the green light becomes, in our sense, merely the emblem of a theme like any other.

Thus we define a *symbol* as a person, a place, a sign, a thing, an act having a larger and more inclusive reference than its explicit meaning; and a *theme* as a *pattern* of meaning conveyed by some formal device.

We may use Fitzgerald's green light as an example of three definitions on as many levels: (A) the device of repetition-and-variation as a vehicle ('repetitive' process, which becomes 'qualitative' process at the point where the narrator reflects that 'the colossal significance of that light had now vanished forever'); (B) Gatsby's romantic hope (the theme, which is also developed in larger ways); and (C) the green light—in itself, and as an emblem of the theme (a symbol).

Such distinctions are, of course, almost purely a convenience for writers, critics and the few choice readers who may be aware of them. In the novel itself, such elements as theme, symbol, viewpoint, process, character are indissoluble from each other, and properly so.

A symbol may be minor (Gatsby's green light), or a major, inclusive one (New York in *Manhattan Transfer*, Paris in *Men of Good Will* and *The Ambassadors*). It may be simple (the letter *A* in *The Scarlet Letter*), or multiple and fluctuant (the white whale in *Moby Dick*, the falcon in *The Pilgrim Hawk*). It may be ambivalent (Lafcadio in *Lafcadio's Adventures*), or magical (the castle in *The Wanderer*), or fabulous (the purse and other objects in *The New Melusina*).

We may say of the symbol that its implications are always wider or deeper—more extensive, more intensive, or both—than the explicit plane of the story. Thus it establishes, by its very presence, two or more distinct levels of meaning.

The symbol may be familiar to the reader before he encounters it in a novel; or it may embody a hitherto unrecognized cluster of experience.

16 tone and key

We speak of *key*, not as a scale related to its tonic, but in the more limited sense of *pitch;* and of *tone* as that 'regularity of vibration' more or less uniform throughout a novel. Both terms, of course, are borrowed from music; and both are of a kind to drive writers about literature to their own sort of genteel despair.

We may do better with a few examples than we might with any attempt at exact definition. Conrad's *Heart of Darkness* is pitched low, and has what is called a 'brooding tone'—a bass chord in G, let us say, slowly repeated. Henry Green's *Concluding* has a noticeable dry tension of pitch, a little above middle C. Its tone is a faint eerie and silvery diminuendo in the high treble. The key of *Huckleberry Finn* is a boy's alto voice, its tone the lonesome guitar-music of a ballad heard from the shore of a dark river. We are somewhat baffled in the attempt to strike a tone or key for Richardson's *Pamela.*

Obviously this will not do. We have no standard of referral. Except for a certain faith in our own comparative taste, we do not know how much of our intimation about tone and key may be conventional, on the one hand, or subjective on the other. We have stretched the musical terms until they are only loosely analogical. The Conrad description is quite evidently conventional. The characterization of the tone of *Concluding* is perhaps the closest and best. The *Huckleberry Finn* seems to be a literal and perhaps falsely poetic association.

Let us try what are called heroic measures. If we attempt to transpose *Pamela* into the tone and key of *Manhattan Transfer,* or *Mrs. Dalloway* into *The Mayor of Casterbridge,* or *White-Jacket* into *Death of a Nobody,* we may glimpse the possibility of a comparative scale in its roughest terms. By placing these books next to each other, we do, at least, make clear the *existence* of tone and key, and move toward a definition in each case. From that point we may proceed to subtler gradations—those, let us say, between *The Root and the Flower* and *The Transposed Heads*—until the whole scale is filled in.

With this imaginary relative scale we must make do for the moment. From it the novelist may tentatively select the approximate pitch and tone of his own book. But he will need to take a dozen other factors into account. If he has a first-person narrator, the personality of this narrator will be very influential in determining key and tone, plus tempo, choice of treatment, and other matters. Conversely, the selection of a narrator will be made in the light of these other considerations. With a third-person viewpoint character, or none at all, the novelist will, of course, have much greater latitude in these directions; but his control of the several elements involved will need to be correspondingly more stringent. If we wished to speak of an ideal situation, we might say that all these matters—subject, key, tone, treatment, viewpoint, tempo, scale, and process— are interactively determined in harmonious balance.

'. . . the unforgivable artistic fault in a novelist,' said Desmond McCarthy, 'is failure to maintain consistency of tone.' [47]

This is a necessary warning, but perhaps it need not be quite so severe. Time and again, Balzac wandered from the tone, with compromising but not entirely disastrous results. There is even a rather unlikely danger that a novelist whose skill is greater than his creative rudeness may overcontrol tone at the expense of other elements. At the risk of being paradoxical, we must point out that tone too must have its *range*. It must be able to encompass the variations of material in a given treatment—not merely in the sense of reducing them to its own limits, but in a way that will realize their full possibilities.

The main difficulty with both tone and key is to strike them in the first place. This is one of the chief hazards of the first fifty pages. It calls for two things, principally: the novelist's sense of what he wants, and his ability to recognize it when he gets it. The recipe is early and tireless rewriting. Once the key and tone have been struck and held long enough to *catch hold*, they will exercise their own compulsive resonance. The novelist need only listen for them.

17 relative scale

This need not detain us long, though it is sometimes a troublesome factor in the novel. The problem of relative scale, as we define the term here, may almost be comprised in a single question: Are the given subject and treatment suitable to the projected length?

This is easier asked than answered. *The Scarlet Letter* and *Death in Venice,* among other novels, were first envisioned as short stories. Their larger lines of growth did not appear until the writers had begun work on them.

But this is not so serious as the opposite case, in which the novelist takes a subject and treatment conceived on the scale of a story—even a long story, or conte—and gives them the full dimensions of a novel. As an example, we may cite *For Whom the Bell Tolls.* Here the climactic event, the demolition of the bridge, is perhaps too slight an incident to support the weight of the preparation it has been given, the relative saliency of the earlier episodes, and the whole mass of the novel. Long before the climax is required, we are impatient to get to it—a sign that, despite the author's overconscientious preparation and the boldness of the antecedent episodes, we sense a discrepancy between the given scale of the subject and its expansive development.

It is a difficult point. How can we speak of an incident as 'too slight'? Have we not agreed that any event is capable of a nearly infinite and infinitely various proliferation? Perhaps we would do better to speak of the novelist's conception of an event rather than the event itself. True, a given event in its context will support only so much development. That word *context* is the key. It is another term for 'the sense of the whole,' and it gives us the hint of our principle.

This 'sense of the whole' is the guardian factor in relative scale. As in the case of *Death in Venice,* it may enlarge itself in accord with the growth of the novelist's view, like an expanding conceptacle; and each event within this conceptacle will show a consonant growth. It is not merely a matter of the mutual proportions and relations between events in a novel. These may be good; but if the individual events tend to grow beyond their conceptacle, or fail to grow as it expands, their disproportion will show itself in certain functional disorders of process. The events of a novel should fit 'the sense of the whole' as an egg fits its shell.

As in most such cases, the preventive remedy will be found in exploration before writing. Here, in the sketched scenes and experimental outlines, the novelist may gauge his proportions and try them out in relation to each other. While he is writing, his attention is intensely and properly fixed, like a scanning eye, on the immediate stream of incident, even though he has also the sense of moving within the whole integument of the work. The skeleton outline will tell him more about the ordering of parts in the whole than he can hope to find out—until it is too late—in the writing itself.

18 character

It is conceivable that we might throw every other element out the window and still have a novel if the people in it were alive. Many an otherwise inconsiderable novel has been lighted up like a theater by the blaze of character inside it.

The term *character* is itself unsatisfactory. Into it we lump all the meanings of consciousness and the unconscious, behavior and potentiality. It is too big a lump to be swallowed whole.

Moreover, it suggests the eighteenth-century notion of *character* as a galaxy of fixed qualities; or the 'characters' of La Bruyère—what we should call personalized types; or the traditional idea of 'a character' as an odd or striking person, which has become a twentieth-century American colloquialism. All these, of course, have been modified and in some respects outmoded by a variety of developments in literature, painting, psychology, and in our own shifting views of personality.

We need mention only a few of these developments: Balzac, Marx and Veblen on man as an economic animal; the disintegrative poetry of Arthur Rimbaud; the pragmatism of William James, Peirce and Dewey; Freud's cardinal researches in the unconscious; Picasso and the surrealist painters; the anthropology of Frazer, Malinowski, Boas, Róheim, Benedict, Wissler and Mead; the typological theories of Jung, Kretschmer, and Jaensch, and the new integrations of the Gestalt school; such novels of collective experience as *Death of A Nobody, U. S. A.* and *The Plague;* and the quantitative analysis of sexual custom by Kinsey, Pomeroy and Martin.

All these, and a bewildering multitude of others, are factors the novelist may hope to take account of. There is good reason to believe that our knowledge of human personality is as yet decidedly coarse, shallow and indistinct. 'I hazard the guess,' said Stevenson, 'that man will ultimately be known for a mere polity of multifarious, incongruous, and independent denizens.' The relatively recent advent of the psychosomatologists offers one instance of this. Another is the curious ability of the human organism to survive the damage of concentration camps and atomic explosion in this most gracious of all centuries. It may be that in some happier time we shall discover capacities for joy as great as those we have demonstrated in the inflicting and endurance of pain and shock.

In the meantime, however, it is not too much to expect that we shall uncover ever larger fields of human personality and bring them into experiential play. In this work the novelist can take a pioneer's role, as he has done so often before. In his ordinary

business as an artist, he will move into fresh country and stake his claims. He will discover outcrops
ignored by other prospectors, and deep veins unsuspected for centuries.

More than that, he will go about his everyday work
of imaginative valuation and revaluation, of connection and disconnection. He may ignore the accepted hierarchy of values in personality and set up
his own counterweighting of values. He may, for
example, choose to exalt the kinesthetic or perceptual at the expense of the cerebral. He may
imagine an emotional or synesthetic virtuoso so accomplished that his very creation will give us an
unexpected view of human life. Moreover, he will
understand that a new counterpoise of values in
personality will have its own enlightening comment
to make on our system of values and our vision of
the world.

From first to last, the novelist is concerned with
character. In the novel, everything is character, just
as everything is tone or process. Each event must
be focused in a human consciousness. Without
someone to look at it, there is no landscape; no idea
without someone to conceive it, and no passion
without persons.

But how does the novelist go about creating a
character?

It is not enough to invent him and push him out
into the world of the novel. It is not enough to give

him a pork-pie hat, large ears and a taste for the music of Dizzy Gillespie. If he is not *there,* the signs and qualities of his passage will lie scattered in the work like the makings of a rag doll some child has abandoned.

We must *produce* him, and we must produce him whole and alive.

We hear a knock at the door. We speculate a little as we answer it. We open the door. Someone is there. Someone we know, or think we may know, or a stranger. Known or unknown, he is a *presence.* He is *there.*

So the novelist must begin with the presence at the door, the whole coherent effect of personality. He begins, not with a part, but with the suggested configuration of a human entity, its bulk and emanation.

The novelist's method of calling up character is a development and intensification of our everyday feeling about the people we know; and he presents his characters by much the same means we are accustomed to use in our ordinary apprehension of personality—the intimations of presence, tone, speech, clothes, gesture, and bodily effect.

If he has an eidetic imagination, the figure may stand before him as the figures of the creation stood before William Blake. If he has not, he will feel the existence and presence of his character, and believe in it, as he believes in and feels the existence of an absent friend.

'Most frequently,' says Stanislavski, 'especially among talented actors, the physical materialization of a character to be created emerges of its own accord once the right inner values have been established.'

A young girl evokes the image of her imaginary and hoped-for sweetheart; a boy projects himself as the hero of a skirmish on Saipan; a woman calls up the figure of a lover she has known. All three are functionally related to the creation of character in the novel.

In the first case, out of certain imaginary persons in literature and dreams, the young girl creates a compounded visionary sweetheart. In the second case, the boy sends out the image of a real person, himself, on an imaginary errand of battle. In the third, the woman evokes the image of an actual but absent person, her lover, and calls him back to her. All these methods, alone or in combination, are the methods of the novelist.

There is a further method, perhaps the most significant one. This is the imaginative integration of new characters from the novelist's fund of percepts about many actual acquaintances. The process appears to resemble (A) the logic and series of other acts of the imagination, and (B) our familiar pattern of realization in getting acquainted with a new friend. The central, organizing intimation of personality comes first. This is at once a core, to which other qualities adhere one after the other, and a circle of reference into which these other qualities can be fitted.

'A character,' says James, 'is interesting as it comes out, and by the process and duration of that emergence; just as a procession is effective by the way it unrolls, turning to a mere mob if it passes at once.' [27]

We may mention a necessary qualification: that emergence should be simultaneous with growth — not merely the growth of a character in the reader's mind, but his growth in *himself*. Thus the revelation of character is no mere assembly of parts, but a stream of becoming, a continuous flowering in which the whole plant goes on growing while each sepal opens.

F. C. Prescott [35A] mentions that characters may be 'intellectually constructed or imaginatively created,' or formed by a combination of both methods. But he suggests that 'the intellectually constructed character will always be inferior,' for obvious reasons.

Beyond these, he distinguishes two main types of created character in literature: the autogenous and the objective. Such distinctions, of course, will hardly be exclusive; they are not much more than indications of the hint or core element in a character's visualization.

Autogenous characters, Prescott writes, may be divided, according to their genesis, into these classes:

(A) A single 'idealization' (we should point out that this may also be 'de-idealization,' in the literal sense) of the author's idea of himself, or of a part of himself, further modified by projection, and made 'composite' by the fact that 'idealization' involves the use of qualities ultimately derived from other persons. This should dispose once and for all of the idea of 'autobiographical' character in fiction —an anonym, as it were, behind which the author hides. Even when the novelist deliberately sets out to represent himself in fiction, and asserts this intention, we cannot credit his account in any literal sense. It is a misconception in terms. There is no fact in the novel. The imaginative process itself must contradict him. We may see the point even more clearly if we move over into the presumable realm of 'fact,' and note the 'factual' untrustworthiness of much autobiography per se.

(B) The dissociation of certain aspects or qualities of the novelist's personality, and their projection as new wholes, as 'two or more characters, parallel to each other and alike in their relations to the author's mind'—though they may also include other features from 'congruous external sources.' Prescott shows how well-defined this process is in imagination, mythology, religion, and in the mental activities of children. 'Thus,' he writes, 'an active imagination will "burgeon" and throw off characters about as freely as a young plant will generate and sprout into leaves and flowers in the spring,—and by a process quite as natural.'

(c) Lamb mentions the writer's faculty of 'making himself many, or reducing many unto himself.' The latter point brings us to Prescott's third order of autogenous character. He cites as an example of this the child who becomes successively a pirate, a cowboy, or a crusader. This is obviously the imaginative type of the actor, and in its extreme reaches, of the pathological impersonator. We may also see its workings in such a novelist as Andreyev, who liked to prepare himself by 'living into' a character and scene he intended to present in fiction. Thus, before he set out to write about sailors and the sea, he took to wearing sailor's gear, rigged up a crow's-nest, and learned to box the compass.

Nor should we forget the intervention of the whole body of fictional characters in literature, and the views of personality they represent, in the formation of new characters.

As a prime example of the 'objective' or nonautog-
enous character, Prescott cites the heroines of the
male novelists. But even here—since our classifica-
tions are not exclusive, and necessarily qualified—
we may perhaps assume that the very indistinctness
of such heroines, frequently enough, reveals their
'autogenous' character. They are, in large part,
projected dream wishes; and their effectiveness may
depend on how much they are modified by external
and solidly observational qualities. 'Sometimes,'
says Prescott, 'the objective character will be a general abstract, without ascertainable antecedents.
Sometimes an actual person will form the nucleus.'
There is a third method, perhaps the major one.
Balzac speaks of following a workman and his wife
one evening on the boulevards. 'Hearing these people,' he writes, 'I was able to adopt their life; I felt
their rags on my back, I walked along with my feet
in their worn-out shoes; their desires, their wants,
all passed into my soul, and my soul passed into
theirs; I was like a man dreaming while he is
awake.' This is evidently an example of the 'empathic' imagination mentioned by Downey. [11]
Certainly, in its embracing of and fusion with the
object, it may well be the dominant imaginative
method of the great objective writers.

As Balzac and others have shown us, there is no
such thing as a character not 'worth' exploiting. If
we seem to feel such 'worthlessness,' the novelist
has chosen a character ineffective in the given con-

text; or there has been some failure of realization on the part of the novelist or reader. Obviously certain characters are more 'promising' than others. But every character, fully and deeply conceived, offers far more chance for development than the novelist can make use of.

As we usually understand it, character is to some extent merely our accustomed context for perceiving it. We expect and receive the conventional signals. We can observe this sharply when we are confronted with such unusual circumstances as the customs of a foreign country, crime, pathological behavior, or some strong internal or group emotion. The 'normal' context is no longer serviceable. We have lost our fixed points of reference—the agreed points of social behavior. If we are traveling in a foreign country, we may cling to our own customs or adopt the strange ones. Usually we compromise a little.

But in the other cases cited, we are likely to feel that 'anything can happen,' and the experience may terrify us. We try to reassert the 'normal' context, to get back to it as quickly as we can, even by refusing to credit the evidence before us, or by a kind of conventional behavior that seems to discredit the evidence. We try to 'act as if nothing had happened.'

These subterfuges are not available to the novelist. He must find some means of grasping such actual or imaginary events of personality; and he must be able to present them, humanized and whole, in terms that the reader will accept.

In the novel, character is inviolable. If we may place one unvarying rule among our exceptionable principles, it is this: once his characters are established, a novelist must be faithful to them. Nothing, no other demand, should be allowed to compromise their effect of complete autonomy. But the potentials of human personality are so flexible and various, so infinitely expansible, that the novelist will find this no hard saying. He may regard it in the light of an opportunity rather than a bar.

19 dialogue

Dialogue is a kind of action, and action is bodily speech. Both are functional aspects of character and the chief means of representing it.

Dickens insisted that 'every word said by his characters was distinctly heard by him'; and de Musset remarked that 'one does not work, one listens.'

These are evidently very definite, though not unusual, examples of the imaginative auditory type [11]. In this respect, the experience of many novelists is perhaps a good deal less salient. There is little reason to doubt the functioning of an 'inner ear' as well as an 'inner eye.' Only the psychologist will be much concerned with dissociating them, though the predominance of one or the other in a particular writer may be both an advantage and a problem.

For most novelists, however, the experience of realizing a character in writing is likely to be homogeneous. The character is present in the lighted field of the imagination, which reproduces all the properties of the actual world—color, sound, taste, scent, touch, nerve tone and kinesthesia. The character moves as a presence and speaks as a presence. He is *there*—but perhaps not usually in the sense of an eidetic figure or a speaker audible, as it were, to the physical ear.

Dialogue is as little a matter of conscious 'invention' as any other aspect of characterization. It is at most a matter of 'persuading' the character to speak, and speak to the point—that is, contribute his part to the required action of the scene or passage.

Thus the role of each character in a novel is to produce the effect of free will under the elastic predestination of the author's scheme. He is like an actor who improvises freely, and in his own person, within the sense of the play.

Considered in this light, the problem of dialogue is mainly a problem of persuasive control. A character should not talk too much or too little in the given circumstances. He must speak in relation to the

other characters, and they to him. Moreover, since
the novelist has taken the trouble to create an encompassing world for him, he is 'natural' in it. He is
no more to be coerced or ordered about than any
other free man. But he is infinitely suggestible; and
as the author changes the conditions of his world, or
his relation to the other characters, he moves to
meet them, and speaks of them, and to them, in his
own voice.

20 narrative

The term *narrative,* like such other terms as *description* and *exposition,* is a survival from those
periods in which all 'thought' was believed to be of
one kind. At the genetic point, such terms make no
distinction between 'voluntary thinking' [35A] – the
characteristic mode of the intellect – and 'associative thinking' – the characteristic mode of the imagination. But this distinction, now more or less taken
for granted, has been recognized since the time of
Hobbes.

Thus, at the goal of thought, such terms also fail to
note the difference between the thinking product
as a fact or concept and the thinking product as
imaginative creation. This accounts for much of
the confusion inherent in the use of such terms. But
as we have seen, the distinction is likely to be relative, though none the less serviceable in defining
major inflections. The two processes of thought do

sometimes interfuse; but the results will tend to be predominantly intellectual, as in mathematics, or predominantly imaginative, as in poetry.

We may notice, even within the limits of this book, how many of the functions of exposition or description or narrative are being reconceived in terms of other elements. Exposition per se hardly survives in the novel, except in the more clumsy examples. Its offices have largely been taken over by a livelier use of character and process. Instead of explaining a point in his own person, the novelist allows his characters to talk it out, or puts them through the actual experience of it. This has two chief advantages: (A) it keeps the action centered inside the book, and inside the consciousness of one or more characters, where it belongs; and (B) it applies our concept of *knowing* as a *becoming* — a concept in which the *process* of knowing becomes as important as, and indispensable to, the result itself. In a certain sense — an especially heightened sense in the novel, where the movement of consciousness is always the prime subject — we may say that the process *is* the result.

Much the same things have been happening to description, in the old sense; and it too has almost entirely disappeared from the competent novel. The principle of the viewpoint character or characters gives us a moving point of selective vision *inside* the story. We may note that Hemingway, in particular, handles this aspect of the novel with acute skill. The dictionary indicates that *description* is a kind of itemizing in space, and *narration* an itemizing in time. More and more these functions tend to merge in the factors of character and process.

In the section called 'Time; Tense: Duration: Pace: Simultaneity,' we may observe how some of the more recondite aspects of narrative have been treated in the sense of their time relations. Thus 'deployable time' is simply a function of deployable narrative; and the other terms in that section may be translated in much the same way. But time is not therefore the governing factor. It is an aspect of subject and of process; and the necessities of these elements will govern the choice of a type of narrative for each book and its parts.

Two major kinds of narrative remain to be discussed: *scene* (James's 'dramatic treatment') and *running narrative* (which corresponds in most respects to James's 'pictorial treatment'). [26] Together, in their various uses, they comprise nearly all the variations of narrative germane to the novel.

The novelistic scene resembles the dramatic scene in concentration of action, and the motion-picture scene in its adaptability to any setting. It has shown itself capable of displaying more thoroughness and subtlety than either. It is the enlarged and intensified view of a situation, often fully detailed, and characteristically short in time span. We may mention such examples as the scene in which Ahab nails the gold piece to the mast in *Moby Dick;* Colbourne's company attacking Port Hudson in *Miss Ravenel's Conversion;* and the churchyard meeting between Elizabeth-Jane and the strange woman in *The Mayor of Casterbridge.*

A scene may be a mere episode, resolved in a few paragraphs, or a situation that requires a score or more pages. One of its qualities is that it brings the viewpoint close to the object—the character or characters. In a stream-of-consciousness section, which may be a sort of absolute scene, we are brought *inside* the object. The usual distinguishing mark of a scene is that it is carried by dialogue, sometimes interior dialogue, and moment-by-moment action. Thus it claims a larger proportion of space, for the action treated, than running narrative.

James believed, in general, that the scenic treatment should be reserved for situations of special import, which might be proportionally emphasized in that way. He himself made excellent use of it on those terms. Other novelists have written whole books as a succession of scenes—*Ulysses* and *Mrs. Dalloway,* among others. In certain cases the writer may interpolate one or more sections of running narrative in the scene, usually as a reminiscence by the viewpoint character. We might assume that an exclusively scenic treatment would confine the novel to a very short duration. This is true in the case of both *Ulysses* and *Mrs. Dalloway,* but it is not an absolute limiting factor. If he is aware of the dangers of too rapid foreshortening, the novelist may even set up a broad duration series and treat it scene by scene.

Running narrative is probably an older type of storytelling than the scene, and capable of more various uses. It is the type of the earliest travelers' tales, and thus originally a factual—or pseudo-factual—account, related as having occurred in past time. Its distinguishing quality is the condensation of many events, and of a relatively long duration, into a short span of narrative.

James spoke of running narrative as 'pictorial.' He worked hard to lessen its traditional distance from the spectator; to bring it into a more immediate time relation with his scenes; and to charge it with touches of warm and vivifying detail. Some of his passages have the muted glow of a decanter of sherry. It may be that he overestimated the prosiness of the older English method, which had its archetype in the novels of Defoe. In any case, the tendency toward a more immediate treatment of running narrative, announced by the French Romantics and carried forward by such novelists as Dickens, Stevenson and Meredith, has since become more or less paramount.

Running narrative has many applications in the novel. Its ability to condense events in time and space is, of course, the chief of these. We have seen that it may take its place, as reminiscence, anticipation or revery, within the time convention of the scene itself. It also functions as a narrative bridge, which may serve as the connective tissue between scenes. It is useful as indirect discourse, a means of bringing dialogue into a short compass while retaining much of its concreteness. The stream-of-consciousness passage may also be a type of running narrative. We have an example, blended with other elements, in the Molly Bloom soliloquy from *Ulysses*.

At one time or another, the novelist has made use of an assortment of minor narrative devices: letters and other documents; the labeled dialogue of the play; songs, slogans, verse and speeches. We may evaluate these only in terms of a particular use. It is perhaps sufficient to remark that they must earn their oddity.

21 viewpoint

The viewpoint character is not always a narrator; but the narrator is necessarily the viewpoint character.

The choice of viewpoint character or narrator is among the three or four most difficult problems in the setting up of a novel.

The explicit or presumptive narrator may be (A)
the author in his own person, speaking as 'I' in his
own person; (B) the author in his own person, as
'omniscient viewpoint,' but speaking *without* reference to himself; (C) the author in his own person,
speaking as 'we,' in the double sense of the journal-
istic 'we' and a 'we' meaning: 'You and I, reader'
(James's earlier usage); (D) the author, speaking
as 'I' or 'we,' and as an otherwise unidentified but
still more or less projected character in his own
book (Thackeray's usage); (E) a character or
characters in the book, speaking as 'I,' and otherwise identified; (F) a character in the book, speaking as both 'I' and 'we,' the 'we' referring to himself
and one or more other persons in the world of the
book.

No novelist has yet contrived an escape from the
presumption that *someone* must tell the story. A
narrator is as indispensable to the novel as a stage
to the drama. Thus we have only two strictly
logical choices: a narrator *outside* the story—the
novelist himself—or a first-person narrator or narrators *inside* the story. Any other presumptive
storyteller is, by our definition, more properly a
viewpoint character. Huck, in *Adventures of Huckleberry Finn,* is the narrator; whereas even Strether,
in *The Ambassadors,* is a viewpoint character, since
the author writes of him in the third person.

We should be aware, of course, that we are talking
about conventions, not actuality. Obviously the

author himself is the ultimate narrator in every case. We are concerned here with his choice of surrogate and the conditions attending that choice.

The novelist as 'I,' in all its forms, has largely gone out of use. The novelist had become an intruder in the self-contained world of his book. In most cases, he could no longer plead, like the oral storyteller, that he had taken part in the events he related, or that he knew the persons who had. More and more, too, he preferred to tell his story as if it were happening in the present, and this added to the difficulty.

His being there at all posited two conventions—the imaginative mixed with the actual—and compromised both. He was like an apparition who ducked in through the lighted window of a house, pointed out the odd behavior of its inhabitants to someone on the lawn, and ducked out again. Moreover, in his own person, he tended to be long-winded, digressive, hortatory, moralistic, and rather capricious about allowing his characters to live their own lives. In short, he was more than likely to be a bore—unless his name happened to be Laurence Sterne or Tobias Smollett.

Thus the novelist was left with two broad alternatives. He could tell his story *without* an explicit narrator or viewpoint character, from the 'omniscient viewpoint'—that is, as if *nobody* were telling it. This allowed him to shift from scene to scene, or character to character, without accounting for transitions. But since this left him without a principle of modulation and viewpoint, or a 'commanding center,' in James's term [26], it also laid him open to all kinds of looseness and overdevelopment. The multiplicity of his subject, uncontrolled by any strong interior principle, constantly threatened its unity.

This was the convention in which all but the most accomplished American novels were still being written at the middle of the twentieth century.

But the novelist had—and has—another alternative. He may place one or more narrators, speaking as 'I,' and employed consecutively or intermittently, *inside* the story. These must have presence and volition; they must 'play their part'; and at the same time they must carry the voice and view of the story. No scene at which they are not present can happen directly in the story, though it may be brought to their notice by any one of a dozen means, from the telephone to the recollections of another character.

But the narrator-character as 'I' will nearly always be singular. The difficulties of employing more than one first-person narrator may well be more than they are worth. Each time he makes a shift from one 'I' narrator to another, the novelist must set up a new panel and indicate the changed identification of 'I' by the most careful and unobtrusive means. Thus the device will tend to be most successful if each narrator is given a large panel—one narrator, say, to each of the four main 'parts' of a book. In general, it is a method to be used only when it is made exigent by the demands of an extraordinary subject.

We should point out here that the combination of one or more 'I' narrators with one or more view-point characters in the third person has little chance of being workable, even in the most ex-perienced hands. It is a mixture of conventions that will almost surely confuse the reader. But here too we can make no rule. Demonstration is the sole test.

In regard to the 'I' narrator, Blackmur notes [26] that Henry James 'bore a little heavily against this most familiar of all narrative methods.' We need to take account of James's objections. In the preface to *The Ambassadors*, speaking of Strether, he writes: 'Had I meanwhile, made him at once hero and his-torian, endowed him with the romantic privilege of the "first person"—the darkest abyss of romance this, inveterately, when enjoyed on the grand scale —variety, and many other queer matters as well, might have been smuggled in by a back door. Suf-fice it, to be brief, that the first person, in the long piece, is a form foredoomed to looseness. . . .'

He argues other disadvantages in the method: (A)
that by allowing other people to tell each other
about Strether, or by allowing him to tell them, he
could avoid 'the large ease of "autobiography"';
(B) that this 'autobiography' would give his hero
'the double privilege of subject and object,' at the
expense of 'certain precious discriminations'; and
(C) that the first person, 'so employed, is addressed
by the author directly to ourselves, his possible
readers. . . .'

We may agree, with Blackmur, that James made
the better choice for *The Ambassadors,* but without also agreeing that his strictures against the 'I'
narrator are always and everywhere applicable. Too
many prime examples, from A*dolphe* to *The Pilgrim Hawk,* rise up to refute him. James does not
'confuse' the factual autobiographer and the 'I' narrator in fiction. He does argue far too much of an
unavoidable identity between them. The 'I' narrator must mind his matters like any other character
in the novel—a little more, in fact, since he has
extraordinary matters to mind. He is not a mere
representative of the author—or need not be. He
can and should be as clearly detached from his
author as any other of the characters.

Moreover, when James suggests that the first person, 'so employed, is addressed by the author directly to . . . his possible readers,' we can only
reply that he appears to lapse, for once, from his

usual and admirable discrimination. If this were so, and to the extent that it happened to be so, the intervention of a fictional narrator would be mere flubdub. We know, alas, that such things *have* happened on occasion. But they do not disturb the principle. They are abuses of it. We repeat that a narrator is 'given,' programmatic, in any work of fiction. In this case, if it is properly managed, the author does not address the reader through his narrator. The narrator himself, as it were, addresses the reader; and he must be as convincing as any other character—more so, perhaps. But since we are able to place him inside the story, we can eat our cake and have it.

Percy Lubbock, in his invaluable book on the procedures of the novel [31], makes a rather brilliant attempt to set up this prejudice of James's as an all-but-exclusive rule. But in his very case in point, *The Ambassadors,* we may discover the signs that appear to compromise his argument, at least on small technical grounds. We note that James occasionally mentions Strether as 'our friend,' or in like terms. To whom does 'our' refer, if not to us— the author and his reader? And is not the author himself his own explicit narrator if he takes us, even by so much, into his friendly confidence?

James's point about the disadvantages of making a character both 'hero and historian,' and thus both subject and object, is well worth remarking. Certainly the conjunction would have been inadvisable, or at least a less favorable choice, for Strether, in that his sensibility is intended to be all but the whole stage of the action. Even in novels having a larger and rougher development, it may still be unsuitable. But there are certainly situations in which it will be clearly the perferred method. We may mention such a bold instance as *Captain Singleton* or such a delicate one as *Lucienne*.

In general, however, we may suggest that the 'I' narrator finds his best uses as a lesser character, fitted by knowledge and temperament to reveal or interpret the action, and so disposed that he may intersect each necessary event at the most favorable angle, place and time.

Several of the points we have made about the narrator apply also to the viewpoint character or characters.

The viewpoint character will be treated in the third person singular. He—or quite as often she, since women, in the novel as in life, make excellent social observers—may be the protagonist, or any major character, or a minor one. His chief functional characteristic—his definition, in fact—is that the *whole* action of the novel, by observation, intimation or report, is conveyed to the reader through him—through his eyes, his awareness, his sensibility, his intelligence. In this sense, he is the substitute or alter ego for a narrator, and can hardly be used in conjunction with one.

The difficulty of employing more than one viewpoint character is not so acute as in the case of multiple narrators, but it is of the same kind. In *Mrs. Dalloway* we may observe how an embarrassment of this sort has been triumphantly mastered. We should note, in particular, the tactics of modulation from character to character, its deft handling, and the employment of the modulation itself as part of a larger effect. The older 'panel' method of setting off each viewpoint character is neatly managed in Hergesheimer's *Java Head*. But the ease or difficulty of treatment is not the test (though James liked the difficulty for its own sake). The problem is always the effect itself, and the means best calculated to achieve it.

What considerations govern the choice of a viewpoint character? These are so broad and diverse that they may be said to include almost all the other aspects of a novel.

(A) Even if the viewpoint character is not one of the major actors, he should be a viable character in his own right, have some business in the story, and be the right person for the job. James made the quality of curiosity one of the requirements in many of his viewpoint characters. This is, of course, a germinal device; but James worked it so hard on occasion that his observers give almost the effect of voyeurism. Other usable qualities in a minor viewpoint character might be a long-time friendship with one or another of the major actors; a personal stake in their affairs; a business or professional relationship, especially of a confidential kind—as a doctor's or lawyer's; a sensibility or empathy or intelligence (James insisted on the particular uses of intelligence) tuned to the key of the situation; or any emotion—the emotion of an unfavored suitor, for example—that draws him into the circle of action.

(B) The viewpoint character should be maneuverable in such a way that he has access, on one ground or another, to all the necessary action, and may by-pass all the nonessential action. The one is as necessary as the other. Indeed, the matter of exclusion defines one of the chief utilities of the viewpoint character. He is a principle of selection. What he does not observe, or get word of, need not be treated. Thus he bears the most delicate functional relationship to the selection and deployment of material, treatment, scene, process, and other factors.

By the same token, his positive uses are even more important. He must *give* us each scene and persuade us through each section of running narrative. He must carry all the promises of process and the shadings of treatment. James [26] speaks of one of his *ficelles*—these are, in effect, confederates of the viewpoint character, and fellow-interpreters of the action—as 'the reader's friend,' in the technical sense in which a lawyer might speak of 'a friend of the court.' In that sense, a viewpoint character— or one, at least, who plays no vital part in the action —is even more directly 'the reader's friend.' That is his major, almost his sole function, except that he must exist as a persuasive person in his own right. The reader will make large demands on his persuasiveness.

It should be noted that the viewpoint character operates as a kind of executive officer for the novelist. But he need not be a surrogate in any other sense. It would be hard to make a case for the idea that young Maisie, in *What Maisie Knew,* is an autogenous vicar for her aging male author, except in the general sense that all of a novelist's characters derive from him. Certainly viewpoint characters have often been used, to some extent, as surrogates for their author's opinions. So have other characters. The practical test is simple. If the character moves and speaks in his own right, the question as to how closely he approximates the author's personality or opinions may well be left to the more naive geneticists of the novel. Unless the author is almost pathologically evasive, he is sure to have given more direct and trustworthy evidence of his personality and opinions in other ways.

We may note certain other qualifications for the viewpoint character. It may be necessary to make the protagonist his own viewpoint character. This would be so, for example, in a story about a Crusoe or a fugitive. At the other extreme, a central character might be revealed by bringing to bear on him, one after another, the observations of every other character he encounters—in effect, the method of the police in tracking down a hunted man. But one of the great functions of the viewpoint character is that he serves 'the sense of the whole.' He himself, in the unity of his consciousness, may be a major part of that organizing principle. Thus any factor that divides or compromises his usefulness in this respect will also tend to violate the coherence of the work.

A viewpoint character may be placed at or near the center of the action, or he may intersect it at any point in, or angle to, the circle of interest. The center may be more favorable for the observation of close psychological interrelations; whereas the periphery will offer the more inclusive and detached view. In *The Ambassadors*, Strether is at the center; in *Lord Jim*, Marlow stands at the farthest periphery of vision. We note that Marlow provides an example of the third-person viewpoint character who may also, at times, function as a virtual 'I' narrator. In general, we may suggest that the 'distance' between the observer and the action will largely influence the degree of 'esthetic detachment' in the work as a whole.

(c) A happy choice of viewpoint character will do much to catch and fix the tone at the outset. The tone of his personality will itself establish a constant, in relation to which the other elements of tone can be arranged. This does not mean that the personal tone of the observer must be harmonious with the dominant tone of the book, in any literal sense. Very often it will be; but it may also be a contrasted tone (a traveler entering a strange town), or even a hostile one (an infantryman moving into a town still occupied by the enemy). One of the stock devices of the American Western story is the appearance of a peaceable and resolute man in an environment of savage violence.

We may remark a few minor variations of viewpoint. One is the 'you' or second-person-singular usage, in which the reader is asked to become the viewpoint character. This may be effective in a motion picture, where the mobility of the camera gives it some air of plausibility; but it is a clumsy mixed convention in the novel. A somewhat different case is the novel framed between two panels, or intercut with several panels, the panels being set off from the major story by a different time scheme and often by different characters. Thus the reader is asked to accept two viewpoints distinct in time and space. Conrad managed this very well in *The Arrow of Gold;* but it tends to become a trick in the hands of lesser writers.

22 extension and intension

These terms require little more than a definition to fit our case. *Extension* refers to the breadth of the novelist's grasp, the height and largeness of his view. *Intension* is meant to comprise such qualities as thoroughness, intensity, and penetrative depth. The eagle's range, and the descent into Avernus. Taken together, they are the boldest marks of a great novelist.

23 levels of meaning

A novel may have as many strata as a geological formation.

The overt subject, or story; the significance of events to the characters themselves, or to each character; the philosophic cargo of the book; the archetypal concurrences with mythology, anthropology, sociology, or dream symbols; the topical or traditional values; the social criticisms implied: — each of these may become a level of meaning in a particular novel.

The novelist himself may not be aware of all of them. Nor does he need to be. But in such a book as Joseph Campbell's *The Hero With a Thousand Faces* he may glimpse the mythical correspondences, ritual memories and psychological patterns that lie hidden in his work. And in such social—or antisocial—matters as the advent of atomic power, he may become conscious of an enlargement and displacement of values that shift the very center of his social world [1].

If he has written out of the full range and depth of his personality, both he and his reader will feel the incidence and effect of meanings deeper than the surface—though the book may be read for its surface and conventional meanings alone, as *Moby Dick* is read in American elementary and high schools.

There is no definite reason to believe, for example, that in *The New Melusina* Goethe set out to write a specific parable about money as magic, or the diminishment of personality in marriage, or brother-and-sister love, or the return to the womb, or the Faustian impulse, or the death and rebirth of the hero. Certainly these are among its meanings; but the charming story of a young man who fell in love with a dwarf and became one himself in order to marry her can be read for the pleasure it gives as a story alone.

In any work, we may search out the meanings that are demonstrably there, and leave to microscopists and pedants the task of reading in those meanings that are not.

24 the conscious controls

'The nature of the control exercised by the artist is difficult to define . . . but the point is that, however he achieves his object, the artist does not allow the potentialities of his medium to manifest themselves aimlessly.' [9]

That is perhaps a backhanded way of putting it; but the remark is central and sound. The conscious effort of the novelist is directed toward the end that the work done may approximate as closely as possible his imaginative conception of it.

We may call this the first major principle of control.

This effort can be divided into three main stages: the preparation, the writing, and the reconsideration. Each will show its characteristic types of control, but each may also contain some admixture or examples of the other types.

In the first stage, until the conception is fully formed and articulated, the novelist will make it his business *not* to control the materials. Once the subject has been chosen (and this choice, of course, is somewhat a matter of judgment), he must keep hands off. The imagination must be allowed to run free, to find its own channels and make its own extravagant combinations. Even if it seems to go completely off the track, there is no harm done. Its divagation may reveal a whole new aspect of the subject. At this point even the wildest absurdity should be encouraged. Like the random skipping of a child, it may bring us to the entrance of some avenue that leads out into country we have not yet glimpsed.

In this first range of preparation, the conscious judgment will be employed, at most, in nudging the discoveries of the imagination toward a more coherent shape. It may also act as a sorting clerk in small matters of names, time and place.

But even here, we may observe, the conscious intelligence begins to play its part as a correlative agent between the novel and the conventions of the actual world.

We may regard this as the second major principle of control.

Once the point of drawing up the major outline has been reached, the critical intelligence comes into full use. It selects, sorts, rearranges and condenses, always in conjunction with the imagination, and in reference to 'the sense of the whole' and the coherence of parts.

When the major outline has been assembled, the critical faculty brings a scrupulous attack to bear on

it. This attack may be comprised in two questions:
(A) Does it promise a homogeneous and effective
realization of the conception? (B) Is it critically
sound in relation to other novels and to the larger
world of reference?

In the second stage, the writing itself, the conscious
control resembles nothing so much as that nice
touch on sheet and tiller that will allow a boat 'to
sail herself.' In its original sense, the term is a true
description of the kinesthetic act. In its application
to the novel it is, of course, far more complex, embracing factors of taste, ear, balance, vision, technical knowledge, and the rest. But the novelist's
sense of it, as he works, is not broken up into these
components. Like the sailor's, it remains predominantly tactile—a feel for what can be done where,
and what cannot be done.

At the final stage, the stage of reconsideration after
the book is finished, the whole critical battery will
be brought to bear again. Passages must be marked
for rewriting, repetitions weeded out, and incon-
sistencies amended. The novelist will search his
MS. from beginning to end for textual errors in
sound, sense or punctuation.

And once more he will ask himself the major questions. Does it come close to realizing his conception
of it? And is it critically sound in relation to other
novels and the larger world of reference?

25 the unconscious
sources

'Psychology,' says Prescott, 'is a science, and even promises, I am told, to become an exact one.' [35A]

But in the shadowy country of the unconscious, we may need the help even of inexact sciences. In any case, the field is so large and indefinite that we can hope to do very little more than point out certain lines of direction.

It is clear that many writers were aware of what is called 'the unconscious' long before Ribot, Freud and other psychologists picked it up.

We may note three instances, chosen from among a crowd of witnesses.

Shelley asserted that poetry derives from 'that imperial faculty whose throne is curtained within the invisible nature of man.' [35A]

'My thoughts drip from my brow like water from a fountain,' said Balzac. 'The process is entirely unconscious.' [53]

'As long as a book would write itself,' said Mark Twain, 'I was a faithful and interested amanuensis and my industry did not flag, but the minute that the book tried to shift to *my* head the labor of contriving its situations, inventing its adventures and conducting its conversations, I put it away and dropped it out of my mind. . . .'

We may presume that this kind of naive self-awareness, often coupled with a neat dogmatic theory derived from one's own experience and habits, has been and is more or less common among novelists. It may indeed, at times, take on a certain superstitious or incantatory quality. The writer bows down and awaits the pleasure of his tiki gods, who will, in their own good time, consent to speak. When they do, he sets down their words.

Nonsense of this sort has led, at its worst, to a rabid division of schools: those who hold that novel-writing is *nothing but* an unconscious flow, and those who assert that it is *nothing but* conscious effort. Both schools are perhaps a little disingenuous. The first may willingly ignore the conscious elements present, out of a temperamental impatience with *all* controls. The second may proceed on the assumption that if the conscious attack is resolute enough, the unconscious will take care of itself.

We may conveniently forget both schools—not merely because they represent extremes, and extremes of bad thinking, but because they fail in any objective approach to the problem.

The evidence itself may lead us to suspect that the writing of a novel involves a great deal of *both*

conscious effort and unconscious flow. The real difficulty lies elsewhere—in the variety, complexity,
and multiplicity of the possible relations between
these two functions. It is probable that the proportion between the conscious and the unconscious
may vary greatly from writer to writer, or even
from book to book by the same writer. Moreover,
the two faculties are likely to be mingled, to some
extent, in each of the acts that produce a novel. The
mere definition of the fluid nature of *consciousness*
and the *unconscious,* not to mention the hypothetical region between, is awkward enough. How, then,
can we lay down dicta and absolutes?

The answer, of course, is that we cannot. In other
parts of this book, we make some attempt to discover the operative relationships between the conscious and unconscious factors in writing. Here we
can only point out a few aspects of the problem and
some of the more workable lines of approach to
them.

Prescott [35A] speaks of 'an associative chain in
which links are forgotten'—the forgotten links, of
course, being the unconscious. Koestler [29] uses
very nearly the same image. 'The common factor
in these phenomena,' he says, 'is an extraconscious
selective operator which selects associative connections of a kind which to the conscious mind appear as spontaneous jumps. Such "intuitive" processes are comparable to a chain submerged in water

with only the first and last link emerging on the surface. . . . The original, and sometimes striking, character of artistic inspiration is due to the fact that in such extraconscious fields association proceeds according to "preferential attunements" which are inhibited in normal, wide-awake cortical thought.' By 'preferential attunements' he means 'affinities of sound or smell, or contiguity in time and space, and so forth.'

This idea, classic enough in psychology, does give us some conception of the process in its simplest form. If we multiply the factor by ten thousand, we may have some notion of the aggregative process of association at work in the development of a novel.

Herbert Read [36] suggests, from a series of tentative correlations between the personality types of children and the kind of art they produce, that the personality type may be a very strong influence in determining the genre of art created—i.e., predominantly naturalistic, rhythmic, 'enumerative,' decorative, impressionist, structural, expressionist, or what not.

If we can accept this idea provisionally for the moment, we may easily find in it a suggestion that the personality type of the novelist may have a great deal of bearing on the *way* he makes use of the unconscious in his work—the type, degree, amount, and method of such use. If he is what Read calls an 'extraverted thinking' type, his conscious energies will perhaps do most of the work. But if he is, for example, an 'introverted feeling' type, a large part of his expression may derive from unconscious sources. Thus the given personality, modified by conscious 'restructuring,' may largely condition the uses of the unconscious; and the problem of the particular novelist becomes the problem of finding what is for him the most 'natural' and favorable method.

26 errors and pitfalls

We may subsume this melancholy subject under topical heads. Many of the topics have been given more detailed treatment elsewhere.

On the Danger of Overemphasis. This is chiefly a generous error of young novelists, who may try too hard and thus place too much pressure on material unsuited to it.

On Self-Expression. Self-expression is for babies and seals, where it can be charming. A novelist's business is to affect the reader. Burke points out that creating emotion in others is quite as much 'self-expression' as projecting our own.

On Learning to Discount Unwanted Intimations. Line by line, the novelist must make his central effect. Beyond that, he must learn to control the collateral implications: to suggest those that he needs, and discount those he does not want.

On a Prohibitive Resistance in the Material. If the writer's most intense effort is barely enough to move the story forward an inch or two, something basic is wrong. He has chosen the wrong subject, or the wrong treatment—perhaps even the wrong profession. Or it may be that he has simply failed to put his material in workable order. Or there is some block in the writer's psyche, a personal clench that projects itself into the book and demands relaxation on its own terms, in the book or out of it.

On Learning to Judge How Much Can Be Left Out. In his anxiety to make sure that the reader will be told everything he needs to know, a young writer may easily underestimate the uses of suggestion and implication. He will do better to overestimate them a little.

On the Dangers of Too Much Improvisation. Here we encounter the manufactured incident and the wanderings away from the subject; the runaway chapter; the psychology-for-its-own-sake and the material-for-its-own-sake.

On Not Working Hard Enough. Go to the ant, thou sluggard.

On Getting Stuck in the Middle. This is usually a fault of insufficient preparation, or of a kind of preparation that failed to solve the problems. The cure is a basic reconsideration of these problems, even if it eventually demands a full rewriting.

On Choosing a Subject Too Large or Too Small For the Given Treatment.

On Overwriting. This is a disorder of the sense of proportion. Usually it indicates a kind of treatment too full, too ornate or too powerful for the material. There is always the chance, however, that it may be nothing more than a difference of opinion on a point of taste.

On Choosing the Wrong Narrator or Viewpoint Character, or Placing Him at the Wrong Point of Intersection to the Subject.

On the Dangers of Too Great Foreshortening. Essentially, this is a kind of condensation so rapid or so abrupt that it offends the reader's sense of what is due to the growth of the subject and the characters. Sometimes it may be traced to ill-considered gaps or drastic summarization in the narrative. But it is perhaps more often an effect than the result of any specific misuse of means. In one way or another, it deprives the reader of developments he had been led to expect.

On the Lack of Preparation. It may not be too much to suggest that more novels fail from the lack of sufficient preparation than from any other single cause.

part two: **the procedures**

'. . . when you have excogitated two or
more human beings out of your own
head and have set them to work in the
narrative (not the dramatic) way, you
have made the novel *in posse,* if not *in
esse. . . .*' [41]

part two: the procedures

1 general axioms

Always the specific in a novel: the scene *seen,* the word *heard,* the deed *done.*

'L'ouvrage est-il bon ou est-il mauvais?' [47]

Boredom is a dangerous weapon. Go well-armed against it.

'I live absolutely like an oyster. My romance is the rock to which I cling, and I know nothing of what is going on in the world.' [14]

'. . . the indefatigable hard work of a great writer:
how he keeps us entertained because something is
always happening, and on the alert because that
something is always changing, and by contrasting
laughter and seriousness, action and thought, keeps
the edge of the emotions always sharp.' [51]

In the writing of a novel, it is a good rule that everything is done to please the reader and nothing
merely to please the writer. The writer has pleased
himself in the choice of subject and treatment.

'. . . that the Novel remains still, under the right
persuasion, the most independent, most elastic,
most prodigious of literary forms.' [26]

2 the toolbox

Paper. Yellow second sheets of the cheapest grade,
size 8½ by 11, may be used for carbons and all
work but the final master copy. It is probably more
convenient, however, to type notes and outlines
on loose-leaf sheets and insert them in a binder.
The master copy, to be delivered to the publisher,
should be typed on ordinary office-grade white, 8½
by 11. Crackle bond and other superior papers are
too heavy and may nick the fingers.

Carbons. It is an idiotic misdemeanor to type any
valuable material without making at least one car-
bon. The history of literature is littered with the

skulls of books lost because the sole MS. copy has been lost: because an absent-minded writer left it on a train, or a house burned down. We may concede the point of human fallibility, plus other acts of God, and make carbons on all necessary occasions. The cost is small, the insurance large.

Writing Instruments. Until sixty or seventy years ago, nearly all novelists put down their work in longhand, with a pencil or pen. (There have been a few cases of writers who were also printers and who composed stick in hand.) Now the typewriter is very generally preferred, though many novelists still favor longhand plus a final typed copy.

Ernest Hemingway has objected that work done on the typewriter has a rigid, fixed quality that makes rewriting difficult. Other novelists will agree with him. The use of the typewriter also has fathered what can only be called 'typewriter style.' This has two distinctive aspects. (A) It tends to be somewhat anonymous in character, deficient in shadings and tonal gradations—a 'public' style, in short. Its internal relations seem to be comparatively mechanical (though this may be a false analogy). Often it conveys the sense of great nervous energy; but it lacks flow. (B) The typewriter tends to produce a syntax plausible enough at first glance, but finally indefensible: phrases and clauses out of their natural order, stiff constructions, etc. This seems to be dictated, in part at least, by the limitations of the instrument itself. Making inserts is a chore. More-over, the typewriter demands construction previously ordered, thought-in-line, whereas the parts of a sentence may evolve out of their natural order in a writer's mind, as afterthoughts, or perhaps as one part suggests another. Thus the typewriter has helped to dictate the vogue of the simple declarative sentence, which tends to reduce even complex relations between ideas or emotions to the implicit and the elementary.

But the typewriter has many advantages too. It saves time—in theory, at least. It produces legible work for the secretary, if the writer is lucky enough to have one. The novelist who can triumph over its idiosyncrasies will be able to by-pass a whole operation: the longhand draft. Too, those presumably jocose and violent phrases used by writers—'hammering away at a typewriter,' and so on—may indicate the release of exasperations and motor impulses which remain largely bottled up in the longhand writer.

The novelist may give up writing, and dictate. Henry James did this, and we have some record of the experience in a book by one of his secretaries. [2] But there is good reason to suppose that the famous later or mandarin style, with its elaborate locutions, may have been predominantly an effect of this dictation. A secretary, no matter how familial or self-effacing, introduces a social element;

whereas writing, like dying, is essentially a private experience.

This objection does not apply, of course, to the use of voice-recording machines. One or another of these may be immensely helpful to the novelist once he has learned the technique of dictation. Wire or tape recorders in particular, with their hour-long spools, immediate playback and quick erasure, promise to be invaluable when the controls have been made a little more convenient. Dumas or Balzac would have shouted with joy at the sight of them.

We must grant that the personal writing habits of each novelist, formed early and surrounded with their own cluster of associations, tend to become more fixed with each novel. Changing them may not be worth the trouble. But in a novelist's heart the hope never dies that somehow, somewhere, a means will be found to make his task a little easier. If he could only write 10,000 flashing words a day, instead of his grim 1,500; if he could only finish the three novels he has planned this year, instead of grinding to finish one:—then, then at last, the world would be his.

The MS. The author's name and address should appear in the upper left-hand corner of the first page. The pages should be numbered consecutively, and each should carry a running head which identifies the author and work. For an American novel, the order of front material (pages preceding the main matter, and separately numbered in Roman numerals, not Arabic) should be: half-title, titles card, title, copyright, dedication, contents.

Reference Books. The novelist needs certain references so conveniently placed that he can pick them out without moving from his chair. A good dictionary comes first. The Merriam *Webster's Collegiate Dictionary* and *The American College Dictionary* are to be preferred. Roget's *Thesaurus* is often indispensable. Fowler's *A Dictionary of Modern English Usage* (its American counterpart, Horwill, is full of straight-faced howlers) may be translated wherever necessary into the more flexible American usage. *A Dictionary of American English on Historical Principles* should help here, but it is expensive and hard to come by. There is always Mr. Mencken. Collins's *Authors' & Printers' Dictionary* is an excellent check for out-of-the-way references, though it too requires a sea change from the British. Wittenberg's *The Protection and Marketing of Literary Property,* dated in certain respects, remains perhaps the best comprehensive reference on the author's business relations and his legal rights and liabilities.

Typographical Style. The novelist may use any style of punctuation or spelling he prefers, *if it is consistent.* He should attach a style sheet to his MS., indicating the basic standard style employed, plus a list of his departures from it. Departures should be clearly described, and examples given. [45]

3 prior attitudes

Once he gets over the aftereffects, a novelist who has finished a book is like a boy out of school.

Now he can *live*.

If he has money enough—or even if he hasn't, quite —he is off to Acapulco or Port-au-Prince. He has a long-blocked charge of motor impulses that will launch him into space like a springboard. He needs to get the fever of the natural world into his blood again.

Of course he will have an excellent pretext. He is going to do research for a novel about a great local painter in Haiti, or a Mexican fisherman.

His publisher, a philosophic man, smiles benignly and wishes him Godspeed.

All the fictions are charmingly observed.

And in any case, the novelist may actually *write* a book about a Haitian painter. Who can tell? Not he, certainly, at this stage.

A bat coming out of a cave, he flaps away into the unbearably brilliant phantasmagoria of the visible world.

He goes places, looks at things, gets drunk, falls in love. The life he had promised himself, in those infinite hours trapped at the writing board or the typewriter—now he can eat it like a dewy mango.

If he regards himself as a man of sense, or if his wife persuades him not to be a fool, he will stay home and bother his friends with too many visits. But it is a nice question whether he would actually be wiser to go or stay.

'I can be myself while I am at work as I am in Moscow,' Tolstoy wrote to his wife, 'but when I have nothing to do I feel that I simply cannot be alone.' [35]

Wisdom for the artist is anything that begets his best work.

'. . . I should go to some warmer climate. But to do that I have neither time nor money.' [14]

In any case, the strength of his impulse, which is a drastic psychosomatic readjustment of balance, will probably lead him into excesses. The intervals between books—these are the times when he gets into trouble, and adds his mite to the legend of the artist's irresponsibility.

Though his manners may be barbarous, there is no safer husband than a novelist at work, and no more impredictable one than a novelist between books.

He takes his trip. Let us say he gets mixed up with a Mexican girl, who has a brother, who has a knife. The novelist requires three stitches in his arm and six or eight in his ego. The girl reviles him. His wife refuses to sleep with him and mumbles bitterly about divorce. He is oppressed by his own idiocy and the unkindness of the world.

'Clumsy Life at her stupid work,' as James said.

Now the impulse has more or less exhausted itself. He begins to brood a little. The question of money, which never quite leaves him, becomes more exigent again. He thinks longingly, as James did at Coronado, of his quiet writing room.

This is the point at which the new book really begins.

But there is no book yet, nor even the ghost of one.

If he is sensible, he goes back to his writing room. He hunts through his notebooks; but all the trails are cold. He reads dozens and scores of books, anything and everything; gluts himself on the alphabet crackers of words. No book impresses him deeply. It is only that he must be fed.

He is restless. He sits up all night. Every scene in a book or a motion picture, no matter how bad it is, touches him with a flick of guilt. Someone else has made something. Life flows away like blood out of a vein and he is making nothing.

He tries out a notion or two, tentative scratches at a sketch. They are no good. The book he abandoned last year? It lies there like a dead animal. He has no connection with it. He wants something fresh. Earnestly he butters his sense of guilt by writing a story or two. They come out very well. He consents to a small access of virtue, and knows that he deceives himself. But he is gratified—a little. The touch is still there.

The big book waits darkly. It has the bulk of a cloud ready to be formed by the wind. The first finger of sun strikes it.

4 the hint

It may begin, like love, with a glance in the street.

Or a memory recovered in all its instant clarity, like the view from a ship's port, long wavering with rain, dried off in vanishing amoebic shapes by the sun. Or a glimpse of other lives, caught at the unguarded instant. Or the edge of a story heard or overheard in an office, a bus, a train, or at a dinner party. [34] Or a general social observation, waiting to be made flesh in the action of involved persons.

Or a phrase in a book, some detail of the illimitable human embroilment, that seems to lead out on a track of its own. Or an emotion—the quickening of spring, or the astringent loss of love, or summer, or a death—that calls for the enactment of living people. Or some abstract fierceness, for liberty or danger or hope, that requires human particularization. Or a mathematical theorem of situation [7]— two wives, two husbands, two sons—for which characters must be found to walk through the formal dance. Or a place, magical or ominous, that suggests its own characteristic peopling. Or a powerful man, a woman so rosy and biting that she can dictate her own sweep of circumstance. Or merely some past instance in the novelist's life, transmuted to his use in fiction.

Anything in the novelist's experience—anything that comes under his mortal eye, or traverses his imagination, or moves crooked in his dreams—may give him the start of his book.

Only two things are required of him at this point. (A) Once he has picked up the seeds that may be useful to him, he must keep them in a dry, cool place—in his memory, or his notebooks, or both. (B) When he has planted a few of them, he must be able to judge which seedling gives the best promise of growth that season.

'. . . the stray suggestion, the wandering word, the vague echo at touch of which the novelist's imagination winces as at the prick of some sharp point: its virtue is all in its needle-like quality, the power to penetrate as finely as possible. This fineness it is that communicates the virus of suggestion. . . .' [26]

What is this but a description of human fertilization —the ovum invaded by the sperm? And what is it but the first step in that long analogue Balzac has drawn, in *Cousin Bette*, between the whole processes of organic and imaginative creation? 'But to produce,' he wrote, 'to bring to birth, to bring up the infant work with labour, to put it to bed full-fed with milk, to take it up again every morning with inexhaustible maternal love, to lick it clean, to dress it a hundred times in lovely garments that it tears up again and again; never to be discouraged by the convulsions of this mad life, and to make of it a living masterpiece that speaks to all eyes in sculpture, or to all minds in literature, to all memories in painting, to all hearts in music—that is the task of execution.'

Or *is* it an analogue—'this intellectual maternal faculty,' as Balzac calls it? Is it not the *same* thing, the *same* faculty—central in women, more peripheral in men—that brings children to birth and nurtures them in love? Are we not perhaps dealing, to some extent, with a more complex manifestation of one of the primary human needs and satisfactions? [1A]

'. . . Not that I quite know indeed what situations
the seeking fabulist does "find"; he seeks them
enough assuredly, but his discoveries are, like those
of the navigator, the chemist, the biologist, scarce
more than alert recognitions. He *comes upon* the
interesting thing as Columbus came upon the isle
of San Salvador, because he had moved in the right
direction for it—also because he knew, with the
encounter, what "making land" then and there
represented.' [26]

We come back to the novelist. He has found his
island. He has heard his chord struck, the chord his
ear awaited. He has come upon his story. It is, let
us say, the story of a small, cautious, systematic
man who has drawn up, before he is twenty, a set
of precise and detailed specifications for the girl he
intends to marry. The novelist puts it down and sits
looking at it.

The process has begun.

5 the conception

Almost at the instant that it touches his imagination, the novelist feels this hint beginning to grow.
So quickly that it appears to be simultaneous with
the hint itself, he has a shadowy sense of the man's
presence, of his *feel* as a person; that he is a New
Englander, or perhaps a York Stater; that he has
a dry, hard sharpness of mind, probably mathe-

matical in bent, but that he is by no means lacking
in sexual passion, though he keeps it well damped
down (indeed, his prospectus for a woman is the
abstract formulation of an intense organic wish);
but chiefly that he has developed, very early, a
rigorous and quiet temper of will that must get
him past every lion in the way.

The novelist begins to put these things down
quickly, as they come to him. In a minute or two
he has imagined the man's early adventures with
girls, his effort to check off their qualities against
the list in his small black notebook (the kind of
notebook in which other young men keep girls' telephone numbers). 'Draws up the list when he is
twenty-five or so—*not* twenty. Wouldn't know
enough at twenty. Or at twenty-five, really. The
list won't stand, but should be *fairly* workable in
later experience. First girls defeats. Bewilder him,
slip away from him. Too quick, too eely. Later—
much later—girl who discovers list in his notebook,
tries deliberately to act *out his* specifications. He
almost marries her, finds out in time. Better to make
him a country Southerner? New England Puritan-
ism hackneyed. No. Country Southerners, even at
their most Calvinist, more realistic about sex-love.
Later, when he's almost forty, meets a woman who
seems to answer all, or almost all, specifications.
(By that time he's willing to concede a point or
two.) Marries her. Discovers that the combination
of qualities he's demanded—plus the ones he *left*

out, the ones he didn't *know* about, or undervalued —make her a kind of monster. What kind? Don't know yet. Must get up specifications first. But his reaction to this is one of big points in book's ending.'

Next the novelist sees that the man must have *some,* even considerable, force and quality. 'Can't be *too* small. That way he'd be just a pawn, comic or pathetic victim, kicked around by experience. Is this a comedy? Yes. In something like Meredith's sense: the education-by-abrasion. Another reason: a really small man perhaps wouldn't be *worth* a novel. No, give him some quality. Also, main point: the idea of his specified woman, good enough in itself, *not* enough or good enough for whole novel. In any case, sounds like a picaresque—one woman after another. Don't want that. Might make just a good long story. The woman business must be part, the central part of his *whole plan* for life. Has the thing all worked out. A little like Fitzgerald's Gatsby. [13] But it's standard-practice, old-line, get-ahead American stuff. Thing that makes this man *go*—get there, in a sense—is the way he matches up so neatly with the mores. His desires, hopes, all almost mathematically conventional. Not romantic, like Gatsby's. But the conventional is *formal* structure of society. Real thing always a lot more fluid and mixed up. That's what he runs into.

'What will he do, with his kind of mind? Securities? Don't really know much about them. No. Some-

thing else. Anyhow he makes money. Doesn't get
really *big*. He wouldn't, except in a very stable
period—through *channels*. But good. A minor big
boy. He's more or less satisfied finally. Enough
money, enough security or control.

'Good point: he makes out as a business man in the
same way he does with women. Gets there, but by
means and ways he hadn't figured, *not* the plan.
Might be effective not to make him just a dull fellow to women. Handsome? Maybe not, but better-
than-average good-looking. He *attracts* women,
even aside from money—more women than attract
him, really. More chance for comedy that way. A
poor boy. Farm boy? No, maybe small-town, back-
country New England. Small lumber-and-coal
man's son? Scrounges and scrapes enough to get to
Harvard. This not so unlikely, even today. Calvinist
tradition about education in back-country NE, even
poorish families send long line of sons to Harvard.
Terrible time in Cambridge, scraping along. Business school later. Seem to see him in business
Boston for awhile, then New York, then all over
the country. Perhaps national organization of some
kind.'

When the novelist wakes up next day, he begins to
brood on a name for the man. Awkward to keep
calling him 'the man.' He thinks of a New England
friend of his: Kingman. 'No, Kingley. All right for
the moment. First name? Nothing old-fashioned

NE—no Aaron or Amos. One of those mother's—
name first names? Something simple. Jones Kingley? Too close to Jonas? No. All right. Make a good
name for his firm. Stet—for the present. But what
does he *mean*? What does Kingley *mean*? Just another poor-boy-makes-good? No. Possible symbolic
value. *Kingley is a symbol of the formal mores in
conflict with the way things really work.* Promising
thematic line.'

The novelist tells the story to his wife. 'Of course
it's pretty crude yet. All stories sound that way
when they're just bare bones.' And as he talks, as
he tells her about what he has discovered so far,
a new point strikes him. 'And there's another girl
who loves Kingley, right from the first. She doesn't
match up with the specifications. All wrong, in fact.
But she's got a will as tough and patient as an old
mule. She waits him out and he finally marries her,
after the specifications woman, the one who's a
monster, has got a divorce.' 'What do you mean by a
monster?' says his wife. 'Oh, it's just a figure of
speech,' he says absently.

His wife praises the story, though she does not
think much of it. She has begun to sleep with him
again. She is glad that he has got back to work. His
work is a rival, but it is better than the rivalry of
another woman.

In the next few days he puts down notes as rapidly
as his hand will work. 'I see that Kingley's quest for

a woman is the old Grail quest, the quest for the Golden Fleece. Comic variation on one of the basic themes. Dreams, mythology, the romances. Hero overcomes a series of obstacles, gains woman or other greatly desired object as reward. Is that why I spoke of specifications woman as "monster"? Probably. Necromancer in disguise. Suppose the loving, patient girl goes along with him all the way? Like a knight's squire who helps him in all his encounters, turns out to be beautiful lady in disguise? Mademoiselle de Maupin. No homosexual intent, but the analogy—squire, unrecognized as beautiful woman—good. His secretary? No, that's been done too many times in the movies. This Arthurian business implicit, of course.

'Some good long lines for the story now. Kingley's search for a specified woman. Mythological figure of Kingley as a questing knight. The patient girl. Kingley as formal mores in conflict with the impredictable dragons of the actual. Calvin Coolidge would have loved him. Note: all kinds of comic possibilities in each *item* of the specifications. Occurs to me that it might end with Kingley going off to a war. Second World War. A major or better, and fortyish. But not chair-borne. A fighting man. Faithful to the mores—to the last. And relieved, in fact (ironic note): because for the first time in his life the formal mores—i.e., the Army—corresponds to the actual. More or less, of course.'

The novelist broods. He broods all his waking day and in the shuttling of dreams, always on the same subject. He becomes that mild and harmless monomaniac, an artist planning a work. 'It is,' said Balzac, 'like smoking magic cigars, like leading the life of a courtesan who pleases only herself' — though he meant it in the derogatory sense, of an artist who plans but does not execute. But it is hard to see how a courtesan who pleased only herself would last very long in her profession; and perhaps that too is what he meant.

Other novelists may begin in other ways. Like James, moving three or four lay figures about in a situation [34] — chessmen or toy soldiers on a board — until he gets the required combination and series of relationships. Or Stevenson, on occasion, working out the story first and placing his people in it. Or Flaubert, beginning (in his conception, though not in the book) with Emma Bovary, vivid at the center of her little provincial vortex. Or Conrad, in one case, introducing the group as a composite character, the crew coming aboard in *The Nigger of the Narcissus*. Or Romains [39], beginning his great work with the provincial express moving in toward the heart of his heroine Paris.

Perhaps there is no single right approach. In any case, the approach will be a function of the novelist's temperament plus his angle of incidence toward the particular work. But each work will present, for him, a special case, requiring its own solution.

This is not to say that there are no principles. *All* the principles are available to him. He must choose.

6 the first outline

In our sense, an outline is not a synopsis—the drastic condensation of a story in story form.

The outline is a program of action: a list of consecutive steps to be taken, materials to be used, themes to be laid out, in the writing of a novel—all in the order of their prospective use, and in the skeleton form of the novel itself.

The first outline resembles nothing so much as the itinerary of a long trip we have never taken before. We know roughly when we are going to start; how much time we have; how many persons are going; where some of them will drop off, and where they will be picked up again; what other persons will join us en route; why we are going to each place along the way; and why we choose one route rather than another. Like the novel, it is a time-space problem. As in the novel, we may plan to travel one leg quickly, and take our time, with many layovers, on a more interesting stage.

But in this first outline for the novel, as in a rough intinerary, there are many things we do not know. We can block out the major divisions in 'books' or 'parts.' We may cut these up into tentative minor divisions—'sections' or 'chapters.' But much of this first outline, like the itinerary, will be provisional. We will find it necessary to use a forcing process— to 'think up' or 'invent' whole stages about which we are yet unsure, in order to fill in the blank areas. Our feeling for proportions, for 'the way it ought to go,' will demand this. Later we may find that some of these 'invented' stages can be put to use. But more often they will be replaced by or converted into something else, something felt out in the slower and more cohesive workings of the imagination.

This first outline is meant to provide a plan that will (A) give some 'sense of the whole,' (B) offer the novelist a chance to experiment with the scale and placement of parts, and (C) make a kind of worksheet on which he can enter, at the proper points, his development of character, themes and other elements. In this sense it has somewhat the same utility as the muralist's first full-scale cartoon.

Let us go back to our novelist and his character Kingley, who has a plan for a wife. The novelist sets a deep left margin on his typewriter and uses double or triple spacing. This will give him room for inserts. He writes:

'BOOK ONE: *Section* 1. Willsboro, Massachusetts. August 1920. Young people's party for Kingley, age 18, and another town youth, the narrator, both leaving to enter Harvard that fall. Narrator one of first families, Kingley not. Take girls home together in narrator's father's Standard car. Stop along the river. Lonesome crickets. End of summer. The small, warm mountains, soon to be lost. Kingley's girl intense, cries. Kingley sympathetic but abstracted, says he has plans. She bitter, says he'll find out life is different.

'Sketch of Kingley's family-town-origins, done running narrative, in month before he leaves. But enough depth to indicate the flinty concentration of Kingley's resolve to make way in world. Kingley's grandfather had gone to Harvard, registered son and grandson at birth. But Kingley's father never got there, scraped fiercely to make it possible for his son. Kingley and father talk night before he leaves.

Section 2. September 1920. Kingley and narrator leave for Harvard at Cambridge, Mass. . . .'

Doggedly the novelist works out his plan to the end, to Kingley's second and final departure—the war, in 1942. He has made discoveries, invented a few names that will not stand. But the story seems cold and flat, as most stories do in outline. It has the look of a chronicle novel—something he does not want. Where are the invested names, simple or

baroque? Where is the whole stir of complex human nonsense that will bring it to life? And where
is the title? He begins to brood again.

7 the title

There is nothing exigent about the choice of a title.
It can be made any time between the first hint of a
book and the sending of the MS. to the printer.

A working title will do.

The novelist will keep an eye out for titles, as he
does for characters' names or the germs of stories.
When something strikes him, he should put it
down. A phrase in a book or song or poem, an apt
remark in conversation, an advertising slogan, some
technical term having an extensible meaning, a line
from the novel itself—all these may provide a title.

A good title usually suggests something more than
its literal meaning—an encompassing vision, an
emotion, a way of life, a period, a quality. The title
is a small bridge between the particularity of a
story and the multiplicity of the audience it sets
out to attract. It may be precisely descriptive or
have only the most tenuous connection with the
novel it names.

The title is (A) a more or less characterizing label,
(B) a trade-mark of the author, (C) an eye-catcher,
(D) a persuasive invitation to open the book, (E)

some indication of the book's general classification and genre.

Certain kinds of title are traditional to a genre. A popular historical novel requires a touch of the flamboyant. A mystery title will contain the word *death* or one of its hundred forced variants; whereas *death* is regarded as being somewhat inauspicious in a standard-fiction title.

One method of finding a title is to keep a list of promising words and phrases. We may add to these until the possibilities seem to be exhausted. It will usually be noticed that the prospective titles fall into groups, each group comprising the variants on a single idea. If we try crossbreeding in each group, and from group to group, the happy combination will usually appear.

Titles are to some extent a matter of fashion. A run of Biblical or Shakespearean titles may give way to colloquial phrases or simple articles-and-nouns. As in other such cases, it may be more advantageous to set a new fashion than to come in on the tail end of one.

This is a matter in which the advice of the editor or publisher will be well worth attending to.

8 the research

In certain ways, the procedures of research for a novel may be a good deal like any other research.

The novelist goes to the library, looks up his subject
and makes notes on it. He talks to specialists in the
field and tries to get a chance to observe its actual
workings in the laboratory, the factory or the office.

But in other respects his research methods will be
unlike the usual ones. His aims are different. He is
not trying to arrive at a disinterested knowledge of
fact—or only incidentally, in order to establish a
milieu, or to give some character an effect of high
competence in his profession. There will be no facts
in the novel, because nothing will have the value
of fact. The novelist is not concerned with the objective and depersonalized fact. His regard is concentrated on the intensely particular and human—
the personal, in its whole rounded envelope of intimations. He is like a faculty wife who talks about
her husband's mathematical discoveries in terms of
his health, his increased salary and prestige, or his
advancement to a full professorship.

Moreover, the writer will be committed to many
kinds of research not usually regarded as scholar-
ship. For example, our novelist who has dedicated
himself to recording Mr. Kingley's buzzings on the
windowpane of the actual will need to do a good
deal of hard research in business statistics and the
methods of the necromancers who practice it. But
he will also try to get a look at Harvard Yard on a
bright October morning, or Commonwealth Avenue in a raw and snowy dusk. He will remember or

discover the general flowering of lipstick about 1920, the hairdo called 'cootie-cages,' and the Scripps-Booth roadsters. He will listen to recollections of the midway crowds on Nassau Street at lunch time in 1928; and he will look for the kind of furniture that must have been used when Kingley's offices on Broad Street were redecorated in the cigar-box 'modern' of 1929.

But the novelist must have a theory of limits. He can spend too much time exploring a subject that interests him, or drown himself in detail. He is faced with the contradictory examples of two great novelists: Flaubert, who all but exhausted the material for each subject, as if he intended to write seven doctorate theses on it; and James, who wanted only enough detail to set his imagination working. Each showed, to some extent, the disadvantages of his method.

Up to a certain point, however, the more a novelist knows, the more substance his imagination will have to work on, and the more chance he will have of finding the odd and happy detail to make a scene come alive. This applies quite as much to the data of psychology or epidemiology as it does to sense detail.

The novelist too, like the scientist, must select his needle of demonstration from the haystack of evidence. But the scientist's needle is a usable common one, and its virtue lies in its being like ten million others. The novelist must hunt for a needle so rare that only that one and no other will serve him.

9 the germination

Now the novel begins to exfoliate in all directions, on some principle of multiple growth out of a single root.

The novelist's imagination is seething. He marks a separate notebook for themes, and another for characters: names, traits, histories, and lines of direction. The main body of his material, as it develops, will go into a series of numbered notebooks, in whatever order it occurs to him. This order may sometimes be significant. He may set down a half-dozen different versions of a scene, and the final useful one may comprise elements from all these versions.

His chief necessities at this point are (A) to let his imagination run freely, even when it appears to be far off the track; and (B) to put everything down.

Our novelist, the biographer of Jones Kingley, will discover soon enough that his first plan for taking Kingley through the hoops of the Twenties, the Thirties and the early Forties would call for a tremendously long novel, tremendous foreshortening, or a very broad and rapid narrative treatment.

He inclines to the last as perhaps more suitable to large social satire, but thinks of combining it with a duration series—say 1920–1922, 1928–1929, 1933–1936 and 1940–1942, all inclusive. He favors these shorter rather than longer panels for several reasons. One is that they will allow him to select typical and diverse social periods, each as a minor climax in Kingley's career. Another is that the shorter gaps between panels will require less recapitulation. A third is that the narrator—who is, perhaps, a biologist—can easily be made to account for these lapses. He is away on a field trip in Brazil, or he is teaching at some remote Western or foreign university. The novelist considers and rejects, among others, the idea of a single, short, highly condensed time segment. He feels that it would lose too many values and require too much indirect narrative.

He makes notes at all hours of the day and keeps a notebook beside his bed at night. The names of characters begin to emerge. He makes changes a dozen times before he gets the clear ring of satiric comedy. Is Ethelind the right name for his hero's persistent admirer? He has not yet worked out the specifications for a wife. In part, the choice of these will depend on the personalities of the women Kingley is to meet later.

Each change—of tone, or action, or time, or character, or viewpoint, or process—calls for consonant adjustments in the other factors. But for the moment, the novelist is not too literally concerned with this. He feels it as a general sense of coherence, but he is much more concerned with keeping things fluid, with allowing them to develop freely in as many directions as possible.

We are already a little tired of Kingley and his nonsense; but not so Kingley's creator. *He* sees things that we do not see, and all his notes and preparations are no more than the gray formulas for his incandescent vision.

10 the working out of themes

A theme is not a technical device in itself. It is material like any other material. But it must be conveyed and exploited by one or more technical vehicles: 'repetitive form,' 'qualitative progression,' or whatever.

As they first occur to the novelist, themes will more often than not have a loosely conceptual character. That is, they will be 'ideas' rather than images, general—in meaning and content—rather than unique. They may be philosophic ('virtue is harmony'), broadly scientific ('life is an infinite collision of molecules'), sociological ('low-income districts tend to favor disease and crime'), poetic ('the sea is the common country of mankind'), historical, psychological—they may derive, in fact, from any possible area of thought or observation, from the emotional to the astrophysical.

But their *general* character makes it necessary to convert them into the *particular* terms of the novel. Thus the procedure in making themes available in a novel becomes a kind of free translation from the general to the concrete—in which, however, the intimations of the general are preserved and sometimes enriched.

The novelist will set down a list of themes as they strike him. Some of these will be *a priori*. The best and most effective, perhaps, will be discoveries made in the business of exploring his material. They will come *out* of it. He will consider which are major, and which require only minor treatment; which are merely separable aspects of his main theme, and which distinct or contrasting themes. He may wish to place his accent boldly on a single theme, or multiply his themes into a net of meanings, in which one may be more or less salient.

He will consider, furthermore, these significant points: (A) how his themes jibe with each other, (B) how they can be crossed and interbred in the development of the story, and (C) whether they can be brought together and securely knotted at the point of climax, in such a way as to augment each other in an effect greater than the sum of their separate effects.

This is asking a great deal, but a novelist must ask at least as much of himself as he hopes to give to the reader.

A simple procedure may be used in the working out of themes. The novelist makes a list headed: THEMES AS CONCEPTS. He develops each theme *as an 'idea,'* keeping in mind its relevance to his novel. When he has considered and revised this list, he makes a second list headed: THEMES AS ACTION. He translates the first list into the terms of the second. That is, he takes each theme from the first list and embodies it as a system or series of *events* in the novel—as character, incident, dialogue, reflection, observation, metaphor, suggestion, or whatever. Later he will piece in this series of events at appropriate points and intervals in his major outline.

11 the arrangement of symbols

Sometimes the writer may invent or imagine symbols, almost as an independent act, and transplant them into the preparatory world of the novel. We may assume that the sanitorium or the mountain top itself in *The Magic Mountain,* or Baron Hulot— that man dedicated to a single inveterate passion for women—in *Cousin Bette,* were largely *a priori* symbols of this kind.

It is possible too that symbolic values may emerge only in the writing itself; or even that the novelist may be no more than faintly aware of them from first to last. If his procedures are the most helpful ones, for him, he will often get, in the way of effects, a good deal more than he has bargained for.

These and other dividends will accrue to the writer who 'knows how to go about things' and who devotes himself intensively to 'staying on the subject.' Effects breed effects.

But the symbol is far more likely to be a discovery made in advance of writing, and *out of the material itself*. This kind of discovery seems to be a function of the associative, analogic or other constructive activity going on in the projected system of the novel —the same activity that brings out the interrelated development of themes, process, character, etc.

But the novel is an art in time-space, and the symbol must *act out* its meanings, turning like a dancer in the spotlight, displaying now one aspect, now another—the archaic line of the skirt, the upthrust regal breasts, the movement like the movement of water—until at last she sinks into a folded and submissive composure. The choreography of the symbol, its line of action, is a theme; and the successive postures in this choreography must finally reveal the symbol fully and in the round. Nor can we think of the symbol as fixed. Its basic character will be stable, an entity; but it will show itself capable of growth both inherent and reflexive.

Let us consult our novelist again, who is in process
of fathering Jones Kingley. He has a title now, *The
Kingley Way*, derived from the slogan a public relations man has thought up for Kingley's statistical
business. The novelist writes steadily in his notebook: 'I see that Kingley is multiple comic symbol
(A) of American success story, (B) of formal mores
in conflict with the actual, (c) of questing hero-
knight who performs labors and overcomes mon-
sters to reach journey's end and the princess. No
continuous development lines yet, but ending seems
OK. The war. Kingley has always dutifully drilled
with the National Guard. War makes him a colonel.
In his war status all three symbolic values come together. Beginning as colonel in war: this American
wartime success story. Point Two: the conventional
and actual mores identical in war-army psychology.
And the questing knight undertakes a final adventure for his beloved—Point Three. Develop the
three lines singly, intertwine at significant points.
Kingley, for example, in both mores line and success line will have whole series of encounters with
'practical' mores of business—actually solves them
in the 'practical' way but rationalizes discrepancy
between putative and working mores. This applies
to his knightly conception of himself too, but to
lesser extent.

'The imaginary woman of specifications a symbol
too: his completely conventional female counterpart. Calls this vision, jocosely, "my Amantha."

When he marries her real counterpart, she turns out to be monster, sorceress—because conventional ideal of American wife-womanhood *is* monstrous. (His mumbling of name "Amantha" in his sleep makes wife suspicious.)

'They have a child? Yes. What would the child be like, for God's sake? Reversal of symbol. Ultraconservative man, ultraconservative woman produce wild, beautiful, organic little girl, wonderfully spontaneous, tremendously sexual. When Kingley and wife, neither of whom has ever strayed, arrange divorce—collusion, hotel-room frameup, adultery (only grounds for divorce New York State)—the little girl somehow finds out (photograph?) and is delighted with this evidence of unsuspected waywardness in her father. His explanation, which she does not believe, only confirms her sense of his fascinating depravity, makes them fellow reprobates, reinforces her little incestuous passion for him—to his horror. Meantime she has become great friends with the faithful-admirer Ethelind—both nice, healthy, organic people. The organic as part of the "actual" mores. Thus both little girl and Ethelind symbols of the actual.'

As the novelist develops such symbols in thematic terms, he notes the development, as incident, at appropriate points in his first outline. The outline begins to look as if ants had got into the ink. It is thickening and changing and growing.

A friend to whom Kingley's novelist tells the story is vaguely reminded of Hawthorne; and our novelist finds the resemblance in Hawthorne's 'Mrs. Bull-frog,' which he had never read. The likeness is faint, but he is pleased. He feels that his notion of certain possibilities in the New England character has been confirmed.

12 the discovery of process

The author of *The Kingley Way* has long since begun to develop the process of his book. Almost from the first, he has been thinking in 'long lines'—a mark of the novelist as distinguished from the short-story writer. He has a subject, themes and symbols, characters, an opening and a close, a duration series.

Gradually he has come to regard the story of Kingley's 'going up in the world' as the *main* line. In one way or another, it pulls all the other elements into its orbit (Kingley's own values as a symbol, his plan for life, the specifications woman, etc.) or acts as an explicit surrogate for them (the Arthurian legend, the formal-versus-actual mores, etc.). So the novelist begins to work out these long lines in Part One. He sees two major events here. Kingley takes a contract he disapproves of, but rationalizes it; and he falls in love, but decides the girl is not for him. 'Remember to keep it boldly and openly satiric. Not too literal, naturalistic. *Some* naturalistic details.

Kingley works like a dog at all kinds of odd jobs—
but chosen for *learning* as well as money. Always
learning. Tremendous research to work out life
plan, woman plan. His darkish room on Commonwealth Avenue lined with charts and graphs: income levels by age groups, etc. His friends—he has
them—find him both comic and impressive. Endless, hard-driven energy, single-tracked. Amiable
about friends' laughter, not at all inferior or superior. (Not suitable for the Gold Coast, but hardly
notices. That will come later, he thinks.) Contrives
to seem the busiest man in school—probably is—
and becomes something of a legend. Always
friendly but mysterious. Never comes out with anything until it's done, a fact. Not a pusher or a poli-
tician, but carries a good deal of prestige. Friends,
even acquaintances, come to him with problems.
He solves them. Learns to play saxophone, little
extra money nights.

'One night a friend, who has a Marmon, extra girl,
takes him home after dance. Girl one of the angry,
hard-drinking rebels of the 1920s. Completely new
to him, horrifies him. He completely new to her, too
—a grind, but not a grind. Blue eyes, lanky, dark
hair. Half a dozen meetings. Fall in love with each
other, but he pulls away, frightened at this unpredictable event. Doesn't see her for two or three
weeks. Involved with public relations deal for a
chain of loan offices—of which, as back-country
farmer stock, he intensely disapproves. Massachu-

setts laws—personal loans—1920s? Must look up.
One day meets this girl Boyleston Street. She angry
that he hasn't called her. Will he take her for a
drink? Says he doesn't have enough money for
speakeasies. "Well, I have," she says, drags him
through back door into room with tables, lined with
embossed corrugated iron painted a dirty chrome.
Table in corner. After three or four ginger-ale high-
balls, she talks into her drink, her nails biting into
his arm. She says: "God damn it, can't you understand how I feel? What are you going to do about
it?" But he sits there, a little frightened, holding to
the one idea: his plan. This is not it. The next week
he signs the public relations contract with the loan
companies, his first big upward step.'

The novelist considers this. Only a little of it is what
he wants, in the form he wants—the speakeasy
scene, for example. Most of it is notes on character
and setting. He has nothing about Ethelind or the
other girls. Kingley's plan is still indistinct. The
loan-company contract has not been worked out in
action. The Arthurian and the mores themes are not
clearly marked; and none of it is bold enough.

Dogged as Kingley himself, he goes to work again.
He develops his life plan in rough detail: the income levels at each age, the cautious reserves, the
diversification, the provisions against loss or adverse
conditions. (These will be important later when
Kingley rides out the Depression of the 1930s.)

Then our novelist sets about the specifications for a woman: family, age, height, weight, health, minimum independent income, politics, and the long list of personality traits. He adds a satiric touch— 'Children: two boys, one girl, at two-year intervals' —and sits back, a little pleased with himself. The woman *is* a monster; and where will Kingley find her?

Our novelist sees that the girl who is in love with Kingley might very well commit suicide in some exhibitionist way. She has been used to getting everything she wants. She is a drinker, unstable, a little hysterical. Why not? He sees Kingley at her grave, with a moderately-priced handful of flowers, in the dreary wet Massachusetts November. Kingley is struck with guilt. More than ever now he must devote himself to the fulfillment of the plan. It is an obligation. It is sacred. It has already cost a life. This is the ending of the first panel.

The novelist attacks each of his consecutive panels in the same way, keeping the main line open and clear. When he finishes, he has developed a good many situations that seem workable. The line is generally true, he thinks, though it will need infinite adjustments. He has all this safely hoarded in his notebooks. But despite his first outline, and these other discoveries, he has not yet worked out the step-by-step series of events that will flesh these situations and bring them to life.

13 process as an imagina-tive procedure

It is easy enough to invent what is called a 'plot'—
an abstract deployment of lay figures shuffled
about in a controlled pattern of relationships. Readers who are familiar with that kind of work will
already have found Kingley's novelist a little dull-
witted and fumbling. Like the moves in chess, 'plotting' is almost purely a function of intellect, of
cleverness. It can become a delightful intellectual
game. Even Henry James [34] indulged in it at a
certain point in the planning of a book—and then
spent all his infinite pains beveling off the corners
of his toy figures, activating their wooden inno-
cence, and otherwise repairing the faults of their
abstract conception.

But we may say, with some assurance, that 'plotting' is not, in the end, good novel-planning or
novel-writing. Though it appears to be more efficient and direct than the long teasing-out process
of the imagination, it is actually less so, except in
the case of the simplest and most stylized popular
novel, where 'plot,' like other elements of the programmatic and familiar, is an *a priori* requirement.

We may mention here that the usefulness of 'plotting' diminishes in ratio to the complexity and
uniqueness of the material. It assumes, moreover,

that only a certain number of situations and combinations, no matter how large, are available to the novelist; whereas we know from the most direct observation of human experience, or even from the casual reading of novels or case histories, that these situations and combinations are virtually infinite, even in a single culture.

We are often prevented from seeing this by the fact that we classify such combinations in advance. When we encounter a fresh one, we dispose of it by slipping it into its prepared order. But the methods of classification and selective abstraction, proper to science, have almost nothing to do with the art or craft of novel-writing. For the novelist, no crab is a crustacean. No situation will be useful but the *particular* situation, no person but *the* person in his unique wholeness. True, the situation or character may sometimes convey secondary typical or other classified meanings, but these remain secondary. We can assure ourselves of this by the easiest possible test: if the situation is not humanly convincing, if the character is not 'real,' we do not care what else they are.

Thus the teasing-out procedures of the imagination, apparently so vague and unsystematic, are actually, judged by the results they give, often more efficient than other methods. They are peculiarly suited to dealing with the thing-in-itself. Two major advantages may be claimed for them. (A) They derive and develop the story out of its particular given material, without interposing the device of abstraction and de-abstraction usual in 'plotting.' The consistently particularized treatment of material tends to produce suitably particularized results. (B) The imaginative development of process is a coherent development, in which the 'sense of the whole'— the interdependence of character and symbol, symbol and event, event and theme—governs each step in the unfolding. Thus, to put it in the simplest way, the novelist will never be faced with the problem of twisting character to suit the 'plot,' or vice versa.

We rejoin Kingley's novelist, who is wrestling, like a general, with the difficulties of his 'long lines.' Into his first outline, now overcrowded with scrawls, he sets the step-by-step situations of Kingley's business development—really his way of life—in the consecutive panels from 1920 to 1942. He considers each step in relation to the other factors. He sees that this main line will require a combination of several kinds of formal process: 'repetitive' (Kingley moves forward from triumph to triumph); 'syllogistic' (each triumph is the 'logical' outgrowth of the preceding ones, and each is a reassertion of the satiric principle, in that it is an ironic comment on Kingley's plan and his sense of the expected conventional); 'qualitative' (we hope that Kingley will have reverses, and he does); cumulative (Kingley's star rises to the ascendant and bursts in a flare—the war).

The line of Kingley's specifications woman, 'repetitive' in most of its development, becomes 'syllogistic' when he marries a woman who fulfills his specifications but finds in her the opposite of what he
had hoped for. The line of the patient Ethelind is
also 'repetitive' plus 'syllogistic,' but in the reverse
sense; from having found in her little that he hoped
for, he discovers in the end that she fulfills all his
unrealized specifications.

The novelist has been startled to discover, in an obscure early French romance,* the story of a knight,
Ilwaine, whose spurning of a girl's love in his youth
had caused her to throw herself into a cage of bears,
where she was torn to pieces. In expiation of his
imagined wrong, Ilwaine swore to carry out the
wishes of a sorceress who promised him happiness
and relief from guilt. Against the advice of his
squire, who nevertheless continued faithful, Ilwaine
carried out her orders in ever more terrible feats of
arms, from the last of which he returned, covered
with wounds, and ran the sorceress through with
his lance. Instantly an unimaginably beautiful
young princess stood before him and spoke to him
in the voice of his squire. He married her in great
happiness, but she demanded one more deed of
arms that would free his people.

The novelist is delighted with this story and its correlatives to his own. Remarkable, he thinks—the
* An imaginary one, of course.

dream-myth symbols of guilt and blood; the deeds required of the hero; the malevolent mother-father aspect of the sorceress, who is also the personage who dispatches the hero on his quest; the hermaphroditic role of the squire, common in dreams; the penis-symbol of the lance.

He identifies the sorceress with Kingley's specifications woman, the imaginary paragon of conventionality who drives him on to acts for which he feels guilt. She is also an infantile wish-dream. When he achieves her, she turns into the monster who represents the malignant aspects of the mother-father image. He slays this monster in his psyche, and with awakened eyes perceives the loveliness of the faithful-squire Ethelind, who in turn requires new deeds of him as the story ends.

The novelist does not intend to develop these correlatives explicitly in his book. But they give him a new symbolic depth, another level of meaning, one more 'long line' of intimations which can be put to a hundred uses. His story is larger than he thought. It is rooted securely in the old dream world of mankind.

14 the discovery of relations

The ability to discover relations between elements in a work is, in a sense, the primary faculty of the novelist.

This analogical faculty, the eye that sees likenesses, parallels, contrasts, series, antitheses and reversals, is in part a gift—a way of looking at the world. But the results it brings, in a more intense interweaving, coherence and articulation of parts, are more often than not the fruits of a concentrated brooding on the work in hand, a searching out of all the conscious possibilities. Such intense familiarization will nearly always produce extra rewards in the happy and apparently fortuitous recombinations of the imagination.

What are these rewards? Sometimes it is as if the imagination had taken two units between which we had perceived no connection and added them to make a sum of three. We do not know where the extra unit came from, but the sum is unquestionable in terms of the only test we can apply: its usefulness to the novel. Some of these discoveries, indeed, may appear so odd that we are inclined to reject them as nonsense—and if our familiarization has not been thorough enough, they may *be* nonsense. But they are always worth pondering. Even if they are not good in themselves, they may lead to something. Theodor Reik has described experiences very like these in the everyday work of an analyst. [37]

Thus we have seen our novelist becoming aware, in the romance of Ilwaine, that his early insight about the specifications woman as a monster, a sorceress, had some meaning. She does represent the malignant mother-father image in Kingley's psyche. But

the novelist's imagination takes him one step farther. It suggests a very strong likeness, in personality and behavior, between Kingley's mother and
both (A) the specifications woman of his notebook
and (B) the actual woman who fulfills these specifications and whom he marries. In that sense, his
conventional mores become an infantile emotional
piety to his mother; and the breaking up of the
marriage an exorcism, in part, of his infantile emotional clench.

The novelist is inclined to be impatient with this.
He has trouble enough as it is. Must he assume that
Kingley has what is called a mother fixation? And
where, in God's name, will *that* lead him—and
Kingley? But the novelist sighs and picks up the
challenge. He sees what, as he tells himself, he
should have seen in the first place: that Kingley's
literal acceptance of the conventional mores is infantile per se. Other people are not so literal. Conventionality of that kind *is,* in a certain sense, piety
toward the mother extended into the whole social
medium. In the frequent conflict between 'making
a success' and 'observing the rules,' Kingley does,
of course, violate the rules. In each case he feels
guilt, and tries to mend the break with rationalization or cynicism. We may observe this same conflict, drastic in our society, in Compton-Burnett's
imaginary children. [7]

But our novelist sees that he is not necessarily committed to the idea of a mother fixation. He suspects

how common it must be in America and weighs the
possibilities of the typical in it. But it seems both
too common and too special for his purpose. Now
that he recognizes its psychological values and correlatives in the story, he can translate these directly
into the general social terms of his satire.

There is a larger sense in which the discovery of
relations may be understood: as the finding out of
relations between the elements and parts of the
novel itself. These relations may be worked out in
the marriage of minor themes; in the crisscrossing
of 'long lines,' or their intermingling in what we
have called symbiotic process. It helps to determine
the apposition of scenes or sections of bridging narrative; the combinations of characters in harmony
or conflict; and the stress and release of successive
actions, controlled by 'the sense of the whole.'

We may say in general that the process of discovery
in structural relations is very much the same as that
we have seen employed in the search for meanings:
a brooding familiarization with the material, plus
the dividends that may accrue in the unearned solutions of the imagination.

15 scene and character

Almost any simple method will take care of the arrangement of notes on scene and character.

Notes for a scene may go into the general note-books. Such notes may be anything from a sentence about a teacup to an overblown draft of the whole scene. Usually a scene evolves in phase after phase, and the order is significant in that each note comprises a modification without much repetition. Thus the more or less final version may need to be a selective assembly of parts, a choice among many versions in the evolutionary order of their setting down.

It is perhaps better to use a separate notebook or worksheets for the list of characters. This should be handy. It will be frequently revised in the preliminary stages and worn to a pulp before the book is finished.

Almost the first thing a character needs is a name. Each name should be typed in caps, with plenty of white space below it for the dossier. Names may come from anywhere and everywhere. In Compton-Burnett's *Two Worlds and their Ways,* there is a family named Firebrace. Firebrace was one of the victorious Sunite generals who signed the treaty of peace with Endymion's Moonites in Lucian's *True History.* Henry James made long lists of promising names for characters, most of them from the London *Times.* [34] In New York, the Manhattan telephone book is a favorite source. Names of every ethnic derivation may be found there, in all the transitional states from the 'greenhorn' to the smugly 'American.' Except perhaps as an innocuous reference to persons 'in the public eye' (who sometimes cause irritation of the retina), the full names of living persons are tabu. This is especially evident, of course, in regard to a fictional character who may resemble the name's actual possessor. Obviously no full name should be lifted from a newspaper or telephone book. The names of actual persons may be used only in recombined forms, and even these offer no guarantee that coincidence or the tricks of memory will not get a writer into trouble. Every novelist needs to be familiar with the conditions governing libel, defamation, and invasion of privacy.

The names of characters should be accordant with the key and tone of the book. This is not to say that a fantasy requires fantastic names. Very simple ones may be more effective, as paradox (the plain man in horrendous circumstances), or as a means of persuading belief. Dickens indulged in broad burlesque placards that remind us of the characters in eighteenth-century comedy. James favored some rather salient compounds: Maria Gostrey, Walter Puddick, Mrs. Weeks Wimbush. Edith Wharton remembered [48] that he would murmur such names 'over and over to himself in a low chant.' He had a favorite imaginary family, 'the Dymmes of Dymchurch, one of whom married a Sparkle, and was the mother of little Scintilla Dymme-Sparkle.' (Like James himself, we are sometimes inclined to underestimate the uses of his grave and mischievous humor.) Fitzgerald's list of the men and women who came to Gatsby's parties is a beautiful period mixture. [13] At first glance only slightly bizarre, it turns out to comprise enough animal, fish and vegetable names to make a second tea party for the Mad Hatter.

The naturalistic naming of characters is perhaps the most difficult of all, if it tries to take precise account of the more delicate social shadings. To some extent, this may be a wasted job in any case, since it depends so largely on the ephemerae of a social context. When this context changes its focus, the book's field of reference may be compromised or lost.

This observation applies with equal strength to other aspects of the novel: to certain kinds of literalism in detail, the assumption of a fixed viewpoint in the reader, dependence on a particular emotional climate or a particular doctrine, and so on. Occasionally, in these matters, the novelist may get an undeserved gift from the future. His period may have a revival in fashion, and the book with it. But more often he will find that a social context taken for granted is a reference eventually lost.

Only what he makes will stand—and not always even that.

In general we may say that the naming of characters is, among other things, a kind of minor sym-

bolization; that it is done by ear and feel; that it
must comport with the main tone and tendency of
the novel; and that it is basically to be regarded as
one function among many in a coherent characterization.

Any name may be changed a dozen times, but its
final form should be settled in advance of writing.
Changing the name of a character once it has been
laced through a book is a miserable job.

The notes on each character should be worked out
as a separate dossier in some standard order. They
cannot be too literal: name, age, height, weight,
color of eyes, color of hair, complexion, distinguishing marks, style of dress, and so on. After that, the
sense of the person, his traits, history, oddities, and
lines of direction, will blossom rapidly. These too
may go through a whole chain of metamorphoses as
the novelist learns to know his actor.

16 the deployment of elements

The deployment of elements on the principle of
reader interest is, in the largest sense, an example
of Burke's 'qualitative progression.' Reader interest
is not, of course, the exclusive governing principle.
The best management of the story requires that certain demands inherent in the material and the
writer's vision of it should be met. But this is per-

haps to beg the question. We may argue that the richest and happiest presentation will also be the most engaging to the reader. In that case we must choose our reader.

Thus the novelist will consider variety, harmony, contrast, and so on in the arrangement of his materials; and he will carry this arrangement through the elements of tone, character, pace, angle of approach, setting, dialogue, and the rest. He will ponder the effective juxtaposition of units as large as whole scenes or as small as the constituents of a paragraph.

The author of *The Kingley Way* will not, to take an elementary example, write a succession of business scenes in Kingley's office. He may give us a full and intense view of Kingley's office in crisis, followed in turn by the quick 'pictorial treatment' of a hunting trip to Maine with the narrator, a business lunch at the Bankers Club, a sad little love scene at second hand, and Kingley's speech before the National Association of Manufacturers.

Even Kingley's business will change and multiply into many branches: from business statistics, to research and poll-taking, to investment promotion, to public relations, to directorships in corporations, to government service in Washington. Each phase will call for new settings, plus various changes in tone and pace; each will be intercut with the other aspects of Kingley's expanding career; and each will be lighted afresh by the biologist-narrator's perpetual astonishment at the intricacies of a world so unlike his own.

A simple novel, homogeneous in tone and setting, may demand more considered ingenuity in the deployment of elements than a story that goes bustling through a dozen decades and locales. Thus the subjects of a Jane Austen may call for more delicate skill in arrangement than the subjects of a Dickens, though a Dickens will need far greater versatility.

17 the calculation of stress and proportion

We have mentioned *stress* as 'the qualitative factor in emphasis,' and *proportion* as 'the quantitative factor in emphasis, defined by its interrelations.' We may perhaps assume an even closer affinity between these factors than that ordinarily shared by all the elements in a novel.

Both stress and proportion are, properly speaking, devices or functions of process. That is, they are vehicles capable of various uses. The novelist can employ them together or singly—even as a choice of alternatives—to produce some required effect.

Thus a 'big' scene may call for weight and intensity (stress) plus a full development (proportion). If it has the quality of intense and simple action, the novelist may choose stress alone, picked out in a very short compass; or if it demands a slow, brooding depth, the expansive emphasis of proportion may be what he needs.

Both factors, of course, have their necessary application on every scale, right down to the smallest scene or incident; but we tend to think of them as applying chiefly to the major pattern, 'the sense of the whole.' James, for example, seems to have considered the question of major proportion in a rather literal sense. 'The first half of a fiction,' he said, 'insists ever on figuring to me as the stage or theatre for the second half, and I have in general given so much space to making the theatre propitious that my halves have too often proved strangely unequal.' And he mentions the 'desperations of ingenuity' required to correct this 'fault,' or to 'mask' it by 'conferring on the false quantity the brave appearance of the true.' He calls the failure to arrive at this proportional center 'the Misplaced Middle.' [26]

It is hard to believe that so acute an analyst of fiction could have intended this mechanistic rule in its literal sense; but believe it we must. It strikes us as merely and arbitrarily conventional; and we may see in it a shadow of James's devotion to the rigid tenets of the stage. Obviously fiction is under no such obligations. How can we split a novel into approximately equal parts—the first for preparation and the second for the main action? Is not the end implicit and announced in the beginning, the beginning in the middle, the middle in the end? Is it not all, in fact, one stream of action? We might even be persuaded to call James's Misplaced Middle the Seesaw Fallacy.

Certainly there is a large sense in which the first part, in whatever proportion, does prepare the second, just as the second is an affirmation and extension of the first. For that matter, no one knew better than James how to employ the effects of a forward and backward play, or even a lateral movement, in time-space. But even if we disregard the actual 'parts' or main divisions of the book—four, or seven, or two, or none—there is a danger in the mere conception of one-part preparation and one-part main action. It suggests a split intention, which may be reflected in a more or less disguised split in the movement of the book itself. We may note, as James did, that something like this happened in two or three of his novels.

We will get a more workable idea of major proportion in the novel if we say that it depends in each case on the material, the subject and the treatment chosen. We may deny that it is ever a matter of arbitrary quantity, and assert that it is always, like the novel itself, a *particular* problem. This is not to reject out of hand James's idea that the novel may

or should have a 'middle.' He himself could not
have been more thoroughly aware that his own danger was overconscientiousness in textual preparation—a noble danger. Against this, perhaps, he set
up the arbitrary concept of the deadline 'middle.'

But even this can be judged truly only in the specific instance. We would find it difficult to set up
even a working principle, other than that each
scene or segment of the novel should be assigned
what it is 'worth' in relation to the other segments—
which is no principle at all, but a mere statement of
the problem. The determination of major proportions *is* a matter of judgment, the slowly experienced judgment of how much there is *in* any given
portion of the material, what it can be used *for,* and
what can be got *out* of it—all in relation to a feeling
for symmetry, an internal symmetry, in the whole.
When these points have been more or less established, a provisional wordage can be set down for
each portion of the book. But here, as in the other
arts, we need not be abashed that it comes down to
a question of the novelist's *feel* for it—like the acro-
bat's feel for the neatness, timing, balance, and
degree of effort required to spin him into the waiting hands of his partner.

Perhaps a good rule of thumb is that the novelist
should not do anything, in planning or execution,
that gives him an unaccountable sense of boredom.
What bores him will certainly bore the reader. It

may be that he is including a certain passage because he thinks it is needed, not because he *feels* this. If that is so, he may be mistaken about the need itself, or about his method of handling it.

James was never tired of praising the virtues of economy, and the prodigies of condensation it demanded of the writer. We may grant him its larger meaning, and even insist on it, without conceding that it is always and everywhere a virtue. It is, at best, an irrelevant criterion, a kind of tradesman's virtue smuggled into the arts. There are times when nothing but a wonderfully opulent prodigality will serve; and if the end of art is 'eloquence,' as Burke suggests, it could hardly be otherwise. But this eloquence must be itself a fuller realization of process than any economy could give us.

The distribution of major stresses in a novel, like the estimate of proportion, is a matter of 'feel' for the material and its treatment; but it is much more closely dependent on the evolution of themes and how they 'come out,' plus other elements. A major climax, for example, will always demand a major stress, though this stress may be of the quietest, even an understatement. But a lesser stress may also be called for at the beginning or at any point in the crescendo. Stress is, in fact, a type of 'qualitative progression' which gets its effect from a whole system of bearing down and release, or of one kind of stress (a bad fright) issuing in another kind (hysterical laughter) of equal intensity, in which the factors of stress and release are combined.

Perhaps the chief problem in the use of stress is that it should be calculated to the tolerance of the elements it conveys. An infantile young girl should not be asked to perform an heroic action unless we have previously been given some intimation of her potential for heroism. If she is, the effect is bathos. Similarly, when a Thomas Wolfe hero boasts grandiloquently of the hundreds of women he has possessed or intends to possess, and the author shows us few or none, the unintentional comic discrepancy is an example of overstress.

18 drawing up the major outline

The major outline is the final one. Having reached this point, the author of *The Kingley Way* feels that he has matters well in hand.

Using the worked-over carcass of his first outline as a guide, he lays out the four main parts of his novel, corresponding to the duration series, by number and title. Then he fills in the numbers and/or titles of the sections under each part heading. He may go over this outline-of-an-outline two or three times, making changes, drawing it together, until he is more or less satisfied with it.

This is, in effect, the table of contents for his major outline.

19 blending the assembled elements

Now our novelist is ready to put his major outline together. He has these sources to work from: (A) his first outline, plus interpolations; (B) the main notes, now typed in numbered pages; (C) his themes-as-action notes; (D) the research notes, plus reference books; (E) his notes on the characters. All these except the character notes he will proceed to work into the frame of his table of contents for the major outline.

He begins at the beginning and sets everything into place in terms of action and the order of action in the book. He uses the page form we have shown for the first outline, or invents a better one. When he comes to the scene of crisis in Kingley's office, he hunts out the successive versions of the scene in his notes, selects the definitive action, phrases, dialogue, etc., and puts them into the outline. If they are too long, he makes a page reference to the notes. He incorporates book-page references in the same way, where they will be needed. He sets in each variation of a theme at a point where it will advance the main movement of the book and still show an affective relationship to the adjoining elements.

As he works, he is aware that this is no job of mechanical assembly. The mere placement of elements in regard to each other creates new effects and suggests still further ones. He discovers minor themes he had not recognized, and his discovery enables him to reorder and point them up. The characters open out. He recognizes new potentialities in them, and takes advantage of these. A passage he had considered somewhat blank flowers suddenly when the right detail appears, a detail he had heretofore recognized only in isolation.

For the first time he has all his materials together in a powerful focus. They light each other up. He works them back and forth, like Ishmael and Queequeg weaving the sword mat. He makes cross references to remind him, and eventually the reader, of the connections between events, themes, persons and symbols.

He *perceives relations;* and in the imaginative perception of relations he makes a world, still in microcosm, out of what had been a mere assortment of materials.

20 the major outline as an experimental model

Our novelist has a model of his book—the major outline. He proceeds to test it as a naval architect might test the model of a new cargo ship.

Is it fit for its work? He asks the questions that every reader will ask. If he is unable to answer these, if he has allowed himself some weakness of character or process or plausibility, he takes steps to amend it.

Then he goes on to more damaging questions. Is the matter too small for the scale? Is it, in fact, a short-story subject blown up into a novelette? Is the construction loose? Do the parts have more saliency than the whole? Or is it, on the contrary, so tightly meshed that it will move with the stiffness of ungreased gears? Does it promise to convey the full meanings he intends to ask of it? Is there some unintentional disproportion he will be forced to correct later? Does some character threaten to run away with it, like an actor stealing a scene? Is the narrator set in the right place at the right time? If the novelist feels that changes are necessary, he will make these changes now, together with compensatory adjustments in other parts.

He will not ask for perfection in the round. There will always be problems incompletely or not quite satisfactorily solved. He will attack these once more, and if they refuse to yield, he will still be confident that they must open out as the story unfolds in the writing.

Once he has done all he can for it within the bounds of his conception, the novelist will test his model in the colder light of the exterior world. How does it promise to compare with other books of its kind? Has the choice of subject been verified by development, or does it now seem a mistake, at least in part?

If he has any considerable doubts, the novelist must make a decision. Should he try to carry it off in the writing, or give it a decent burial in his files? He has a sizable investment in it now, but far less than if he had tried to write the book and been forced to abandon it. If he is sure that his doubts are not a matter of temporary depression, the answer is clear. He should put it away and look at it again in a year or two. The mere strength of his doubt offers a sufficient contraindication to writing this book at the moment.

But if the outline pleases him, if it lies glimmering with promise on the page, like a summer morning waiting to be used, he has only to go ahead.

21 the major outline as a reference

We have seen the uses of the major outline as an imaginative exploration, a record of such exploration, a clearing house where balances are adjusted, and an experimental model to be tested in advance of writing.

It has, however, a more immediate and practical use. It is at once an epitome of references and an agenda for the day's work.

Thus, when the novelist sits down to work, he does not stare at a blank page and a scene unrealized. He has something to go on. He has, first, the immense confidence derived from his knowledge that the road has been surveyed, laid out and roughly graded. Moreover, he knows where he is going. He has the topographical map before him. He can be confident that today's work leads out of yesterday's and into tomorrow's. This sense of a planned continuity of effort will be almost as valuable to him as the survey itself.

Second, the major outline will pay for itself as a systematic time-saver. The novelist, or any other artist, need not shrug off this notion of time-saving as the concept of a business culture. Business culture or not, he is obscurely caught in it, as he well knows, and remotely subject to its modes of being. Precisely because his work, even with the most thorough preparation, is seemingly less 'efficient' than other kinds of work, more liable to unpredictable and exasperating blocks, he needs to clarify it as much as he can. Art is still *ars longa,* and life is short. It behooves him to get as much good work done as he can.

If the novelist finds that systematic preparation of this kind interferes with his best work, then he should, of course, reject it. It may be strongly anti-pathetic to his temperament, or it may get in the way of a method he has found more valuable, for him. Or again, he may regard writing as a Delphic voice speaking through him. In that case, all inter-ference with the voice becomes an impiety. It is easy enough to lampoon the idea of 'inspiration' on rationalist grounds. Certainly it has often been harmful in literature, as regards things done and things not done. We have seen, however, that there is a good deal to be said for it in the particular sense of an unconscious flow.

But more often than not, a dislike for thorough cul-tivation is simply an impatience with what appears to be extra and avoidable work. A teacher of novel-writing once mentioned to an experienced editor-critic the difficulty of trying to persuade student novelists that a book needs rigorous preparation. The critic nodded. 'I know,' he said. 'Lazy. Just plain lazy.'

The novelist who has drawn up a major outline will have the day's agenda before him. He need not lose time hunting a reference through half a dozen books, trying to remember an apt phrase or snatch of dialogue, or worrying about whether some aspect of his scene will comport with another scene not yet written. Given the natural reluctance to begin writ-ing, this kind of thing can end in a working day half wasted. But our novelist has everything in hand.

He reads over the outline of the scene. He looks up
the references to sections of this scene in his notes.
He goes over the page references in books and lays
these out where he can get at them. He is ready to
go to work.

22 the allowance for improvisation

We have mentioned two types of improvisation in
the novel: (A) a forced invention, which results in
effects having only a surface plausibility; (B) a
runaway extemporization, which inflates one part
or another in monstrous disproportion to the whole.

But there are other kinds of improvisation, in the
sense of spontaneous and unplanned effects.
Though James comes close to it, we should find it
ridiculous to argue that improvisation has no place
in the novel. Indeed, the whole problem of improvisation, its nature, degree and relative quantity, is
one of the more fascinating mysteries of literature.
In a broad sense, it is involved with the problems of
imagination and the unconscious. In its narrower
reference, it is one of the chief factors governing the
effect of autonomy and spontaneity in a novel.
More than that, it is the bearer of those unexpected
gifts of the imagination which no novelist can afford
to reject.

But what strikes us at once is the sense of an undeclared conflict between the planned process of a

novel and the impulse toward free improvisation. Carried out to the last decimal of the absolute, there *is* perhaps such a conflict. But reduced to workable terms, it becomes a favorable and controlled tension.

What are these terms? We may understand them better if we think of our planned process, not as a frame or mold into which the materials must be fitted, but as an interwoven series of magnetic lines of force having a definite extension in time and space. The energy in these lines of force is contractive. They tend to draw the events of the novel into their field of influence. The energy of free improvisation is expansive. It tends to fly off from the lines of force. The problem of the novelist is to control these two energies in a continuous and balanced tension that will allow the freest play of imaginative improvisation along these previously imagined lines of direction.

At its happiest, this tension can produce results so extraordinary that the novelist himself may not be immediately or fully aware of them. Intractable materials will take shape and fall into line. A whole sequence of technical events, beautifully consonant with the major process, will as it were produce themselves without conscious direction from him. As Burke puts it, but in a somewhat more extended sense, he is 'talking on the subject.' He is like an extempore speaker who, having chosen his topic and the best approach to it, finds himself saying perfectly germane things as new to him as they are to his audience.

How can the novelist strike and hold the most effective tension between process and improvisation? It may be that such a question can be answered only in terms of a particular writer and a particular book. Perhaps it is largely a matter of experience operating as a kind of tactile control. Certainly the desirable ratio between process and improvisation will vary from book to book.

A free-running picaresque, such as *Huckleberry Finn,* in which a generous improvisation is the heart of the matter, would be compromised by the dense articulation of process in *What Maisie Knew* or *Death in Venice.* Even so, we may glimpse a warning in the famous botched and 'plotted' ending of *Huckleberry Finn,* which resembles nothing so much as a child, anxious and accused, trying to talk himself out of a lie in which he has wholly believed. Improvisation alone is not enough; and process alone is not enough, we may suggest, in such a novel as *The Golden Bowl.*

It is difficult to lay down a working axiom that will define the optimum relative proportions of the two elements in each case. We may say, in general, that most novelists would do well to err a little on the side of process; the usual tendency is all in the other direction. But if it is difficult to make a positive definition, the negative is far less so. Any novelist should be able to recognize the signals. An errant improvisation will announce itself in looseness, irrelevance, a wandering away from the subject, and particularly in a megalomelia of parts. Process too literally adhered to will be evident in a certain bareness, a sharpness of angles, an uncomfortable stricture. It will tend to reveal a lack of fluency, of graceful transitions, the spontaneous and casual, or the odd note of unexpected insight.

But the pathological dominance of process is rare indeed. We can suggest only two typical cases: (A) the word-costive amateur, who has 'plotted' his story so heavily that he can find almost nothing to add to it; and (B) the tired hack or professional technician, who can no longer produce the flesh for his bones of action.

23 variant types of approach

Long before this point has been reached, almost any working novelist who has honored us so far will be roaring in his beard.

He will lecture his friends. He will warn away younger writers. We are anathema. What? No 'fact' in a novel? No description? No plot? And character is a 'doubtful' word? He will have us know that he has earned his living for twenty years with just these things, and he does not doubt it is a better living than ours. (We do not doubt it either.)

Or, if he belongs to another school, he will whiten a little at the notion of lumping the romance with the novel proper—or at the idea that the technical ground gained since the middle of the nineteenth century should be compromised by 'loose standards.' What then becomes of the idea of progress? If we mention that hardly anyone has written a better novel, in its way, than *Gargantua* or *Don Quixote* or *Pride and Prejudice,* he will feel that we are belaboring him with great exceptions.

But he is perhaps most outraged at our attempt to lay down an arbitrary theory of method. He himself, without a word of preparation, writes his novels backwards from end to beginning; and is he not the author of *Winderby's Trumpet* and *The Color of Heaven?* His friend George McGillivray begins in the middle and fans out to either end. William Tither dictates three novels at once—a sentence to each, impartially—at the rate of 3,000 words a minute.

We can only reply, as composedly as we may, that our guest has his facts in order. The evidence is against us. We too believe in the Bill of Rights. We too believe most devotedly that every man is entitled to his own method. It works for him, and there are perhaps deep temperamental reasons why this should be so. Beyond these, the hypnotic effect of certain habits should not be discounted. They may play more part in composition than any systematic attack could do. The opposition, in fact, is false. Habits *are* systematic, for a particular writer, and he violates them at his peril.

The only possible test is the work produced, its amount and quality. Even this may be complicated by so many gratuitous factors, from the birth of a child to the loss of a bank account, that it offers no fair test of method—though it may be a test of other qualities.

But we suggest that there may be an inclusive and archetypal method—roughly the method we have detailed above—and that this may be used as a yardstick. When all the other aspects have been balanced, including the untouchable factor of temperament, it may still be possible to conclude that certain procedures are less wasteful than others. We are trying to arrive at a method that will be at once least wasteful and most hospitable to the variations of the individual writer.

Let us consider the case of a novelist who writes a rough first draft of his book with only the scantiest preparation. He is, in effect, trying to make this draft serve the various purposes of outline, imaginative exploration, development of themes, process, and the rest. We submit that, sentence for sentence, he is doing more work and getting less for his labor than our novelist who makes a plan in advance. The rough-draft novelist goes through the same basic procedure, but in a more wasteful way.

There is another kind of novelist who makes few notes but who works his subject out in advance— 'in his head,' as he says. We observe that his essential procedure is the same as our novelist's—that is, an intensive advance preparation of the material— but that it is not written down. Offhand, this would seem to by-pass a good many operations and thus to be far less wasteful. It is, if the writer has a brilliant and infallible memory, an immense grasp of relationships, and a rather simple story to tell. Some novelists do combine these specifications, and we salute them.

But for others the procedure has many and appalling difficulties. The minor aspects of a scene have not been matured in the imagination, and must be improvised. For some writers, as we have seen, improvisation is a forcing process, and its results will have only a shallow plausibility. For others, it becomes a loose and wayward gallop, off from the main body of the wagon train, into lost hills at nightfall. Thomas Wolfe will provide examples of this.

There are further and more subtle perplexities. The novelist who plans 'in his head' may remember *what* he planned to do, in a certain instance, but not *why* — *why*, that is, he made this choice among a hundred. Thus the choice may seem arbitrary and less than exigent. He will feel free to make another, more attractive at the moment. But when he does, he may find that he has disturbed a whole internal system of relationships. He must make a series of compensatory adjustments. Sometimes, even when a work has been well and thoroughly planned, a new alternative may offer so many advantages that this kind of change will be necessary; but it should be made with all the evidence in hand, and a full view of its consequences.

Moreover, the distress of the novelist who prepares things 'in his head' will increase in apparent ratio to the complexity of his subject and the thoroughness with which he exploits it. There will be a point of complexity beyond which he cannot go. It is not hard to see why this should happen. We may perhaps be allowed such 'practical' analogies as the building of a bridge, or the design and construction of an airplane. These, like the planning and composition of a novel, require the solution of thousands of individual problems; and each solution must be finally related to all the others. The airplane offers a particularly good parallel. The first sketches, which correspond to our preliminary outline; the multitude of blueprints and corrected blueprints for each part, which resemble our working and reworking of scenes, symbols and themes in the notebooks; the mockup, which incorporates and consolidates these parts, as our major outline does, and is itself capable of being reworked—all these have their suggestive value. Nor can we argue with any color of certainty that the novel is purely a work of the imagination and the airplane nothing but applied engineering. As we have noted, further research in the functions of the imagination may lead us to discover that the operations series at work in the designing of an airplane or a novel do not merely resemble each other. They may be the *same* process, applied to quite different materials, under different principles of procedure, and to different ends.

24 the writing begins

Happy the novelist who has found an opening paragraph before he begins to write.

Who shall say how a novel should begin? Like *Maggie:* 'A very little boy stood upon a heap of gravel for the honour of Rum Alley'? Or, like *Anna Karenina,* with an apothegm: 'Happy families are all alike; every unhappy family is unhappy in its own way'? Or like Constant's *Adolphe:* 'In my twenty-third year I had completed my studies at Gottingen'? Or like its descendant, *The Devil in The Flesh:* 'I am about to lay myself open to many reproaches'? Or like *Pamela:* 'Dear Father and Mother, I have great trouble, and some comfort, to acquaint you with'? Or like *The Sorrows of Young Werther:* 'How glad I am to have got away'? Or like *Moby Dick:* 'Call me Ishmael.' Or like *The Pastoral Symphony:* 'The snow has been falling continuously for the last three days and all the roads are blocked'? Or like *The Bostonians:* ' "Olive will come down in about ten minutes; she told me to tell you that" '? Or like any dozen English, French, Italian or American novels of the nineteenth century: 'At the end of a calm midsummer afternoon in 18—, a solitary carriage drawn by two dappled horses might have been seen wending its way toward . . . '?

What do these openings have in common? Very little, except that they are all intended to arouse interest, and some, at least, do. They are meant to buttonhole the reader, in one way or another, and detain him for those few moments the writer needs to get the story started. If they are apt, they strike a key and hint at promises to come. Tolstoy's is like a long opening chord. Melville's has a somber composure, the composure of the self-determined outcast who claims his own tradition. Gide's is touched with a waiting sensibility, secrecy, loneliness, the fire in the snow. Or do we read these things into them, in some measure, after we have read the book?

In any case, whether the opening is pseudofactual or poetic, enigmatic or limpid, a conventional 'beginning' or a designedly casual one, the problem is the same: to get things started. If we try to be any more specific than that, the exceptions rise in a cloud. It is not even a matter of *where* to start. In the opening paragraph or page, we may not be concerned with the story at all in any direct sense. We are beating up a rumor, like the parade drummer's ruffle and flourish before the band begins.

But the band *does* begin; and from that point on the novelist has his work cut out for him. In a sense—technically, at least—the first fifty pages may be the hardest. It will seem to him, in these beginning moments, that everything must be done at once. He must strike the key and hold it steadily through the opening passages. This alone may call for a dozen rewritings. Each theme must be anchored firmly and in order, like the pier of a bridge from which the cables will be strung. Symbols must be laid out, and the characters set moving in their own autonomy of being.

In those first fifty pages or so, nearly all the promises, explicit or intimated, must be given to the reader—promises that will sometimes lead into other promises, often on different terms, like a business note renewed. The power and persuasiveness of these inducements are intended to solicit the reader's interest, not merely in how things *come out*, but in how they *unfold*. On these promises, chiefly, the degree and intensity of his involvement will depend. But how are these things done? The only possible answer is 'naturally'—that is, in a way that seems 'natural' to the key, the subject, and the kind of treatment chosen. But this requires large qualifications. The 'conventional form' opening can be adapted to a variety of subjects. The opening of a fantasy may need to be as 'unnatural' as possible, in the literal sense, but still 'natural' to its subject. Among all the definitions of 'natural' we may perhaps claim only one: 'proper to the circumstances of the case.'

Every teacher of writing will be familiar with certain stock questions. 'Should a character be described fully on his entrance, or should he be developed little by little?' The question is sufficiently answered in James's remark, heretofore cited, to the effect that the gradual revelation of character is itself part of the formal process. 'Should the story open with dialogue, action, preparation or description?' It needs to open in key; and whatever else it may do depends on the novelist's judgment of the particular instance.

In any case, we can be sure that these are vain questions, conceived on too short a scale of reference. How can the best treatment of character be gauged without reference to the interlinked themes, process or tone? More than that, such questions demand rules of thumb that would inhibit the writer's free choice of means; and they suggest the substitution of some vague or 'standard' authority for this free choice. But there is no substitute for the novelist's self-reliance, and no authority superior to it in his work. There are no *musts*. There are no rules. There is only a cluster of more or less well-understood principles, any one of which may be violated or transcended by the novelist who can do better in *his* particular case.

What *has* been done is freely displayed in all the novels of the world. But what *can* be done is limited only by the novelist's powers of demonstration.

One more point must be noted here. Before the novelist begins to write, he needs to put the very terms of the technical apparatus we have been discussing out of his mind. He has already translated them into the useful correlatives of movement in his outline. They are concepts, generalizations. Hereafter he will deal only in particulars. The terms can be no more use to him. They may actually get in his way. Moreover, like all effective learning, they have been converted into active patterns of mind. He may trust these patterns. They are the operative equivalent of what he has learned.

Theodor Reik makes the same point in regard to an analyst beginning to practice. He uses the example of a young actor in his first role. 'The actor should, when he walks out upon the stage, forget what he has studied at the academy. He must brush it aside as if it had never been there. . . . What he has

been taught has by now reached tissues so deep—
and I mean this literally: his nerve tissues in both
brain and body—that he can afford to act as if he
had never seen the inside of a dramatic academy.'
[37]

25 the daily attack

'It is time to return to the Bovary,' Flaubert would
say, tapping out his clay pipe in the little back pa-
vilion under the willows at Croisset. 'The Bovary?
What was that?' said his niece, Caroline Commanville, long afterwards. 'I didn't know. But I respected the name, those two words, as I respected
everything that came from my uncle, and believed
vaguely that it was a synonym for work, and work
was writing, as was well understood.' [6]

There is a kind of capillary action in the daily flow
of narrative. Some of this is habit. Some of it is a
demanding absorption in the unfolding world of the
novel. But perhaps the most significant part is what
may be called an attractive function of the imagination, a function that seems to draw each day's
work out of the preceding day's and into the next.
Sometimes, for example, the writer may get himself
started by copying the last two or three pages of the
previous day's work, even when this work is already satisfactory.

The novelist must take advantage of these factors.
The first, of course, is habit. He will discover the

most favorable working hours, for him. Once he has
done this, he must see to it that he is moored to his
chair every day during those hours. This requires a
considerable effort—sometimes outright bullying—
by the superego. He will take himself by the back
of the neck and see that it is done. There is no way
to do it but to do it. He may, however, bribe himself
with promises of what he will do later.

Consider Balzac settling down to work, as Stefan
Zweig shows him in the superb chapter called
'Black Coffee.' 'He leaned back in his chair rolled
back the sleeve of his robe to allow free play to his
right hand. Then he spurred himself on with half-
jesting remarks addressed to himself, like a coach-
man encouraging his horses to pull on the shafts.
Or he might have been compared to a swimmer
stretching his arms and easing his joints before taking the steep plunge from the diving-board.' [53]

Or Tolstoy, putting off the grim moment. 'With one
hand stuck in his leather belt and with a full glass
of tea in the other, he stood by the door for hours,
talking with glee and animation. At last he went to
work. . . . Until three or four in the afternoon
complete quiet reigned in the house. "Lev is at
work!" Then he came out of his study, went for a
walk or a swim.' [35]

As he gets into the book the novelist will find himself being absorbed little by little into the imaginary
world he is creating. 'His day was the small circle

of light cast by the candles, and he was aware of neither space nor time, but only of the world that he was himself fashioning.' [53] Even when he is not at work, the problem of little Janie Norton's relation to Jones Kingley will come between him and the newspaper he is looking at. A bright cloud of his imaginary creatures will move before his eyes as he falls asleep. They will be with him when he wakes up. Often his best insights will come crowding at that hour and must be put down before they escape. The notebook at his bedside will catch his often irrecoverable night thoughts.

He will find too that, even while he is engaged on one scene, his imagination, aware of the scenes that have come before, is also feeling its way into yet other scenes ahead. The novelist will enter such anticipations in the major outline. But he will notice that his imagination tends to concentrate on the section immediately following. Even when he has finished work for the day, the imagination will go on producing details—phrases, fragments of talk, aspects of light on snow. If he will put these down as notes for the next day's work, they may help to take some of the strain off each new beginning.

26 'the stream of composition'

Each day the writing must begin again, like the endless task of Sisyphus.

The novelist is like that old Corinthian King in Hades, condemned forever to push a great rock, weightier than his own body, up the hill. With every inch he gains, the rock grows heavier, the pitch steeper.

Each time, for Sisyphus, when he had almost gained the crest, the rock rolled back and he must begin again. The novelist too must begin again each time, but he is luckier than Sisyphus. Each time, if he tries hard enough, *his* rock *does* go over the crest and roll down the other slope, so easily that it seems to him he can guide it like a boy's hoop. Then he must keep it going until it loses momentum and stops at last.

This is one of the major secrets in the composition of prose narrative.

Let us put it another way. The novelist, when he begins work, is a man caught in a locked room. He has promised to perform some urgent task in the world outside. The room is so narrow that he cannot lunge at the door. He must put his shoulder to it and thrust harder and harder until the lock breaks, the wood splinters, and he is out, running free in strong sunlight. He goes on toward the goal he has set, the far mountain, until his stride fails and the breath comes like fire in his lungs.

The breaking through is like the phenomenon of an athlete's second wind.

The onset of fatigue can be detected in the appearance of broad, loose, hollow sentences, like the sprawling stride of a runner as his strength begins to fade.

The rock of Sisyphus, the locked door—these are the novelist's conscious self. The task, like any great task, calls for an act of self-abandonment, and self-abandonment is anguish until it is made good. After that the *whole* man comes into play, he is released in his own custody, and all his faculties move beautifully together like the body of a dancer.

At its worst, this task of breaking through may have a quality of dark and frightening anguish. All self-abandonment—in war, religion, motherhood, love, old age—must be frightening. But it is a deep law of fulfillment.

Literature is no country for the timid.

Sisyphus, however, may borrow a lever from Archimedes. The best lever, again, is habit. The novelist who writes every day, on the same task or varied ones, will not find it quite so hard to break down the door each time. It may be that there is even a definite ratio between the difficulty and the lapse of time from writing to writing. He must allow for recuperation, of course. But in general, the shorter the lapse, the more quickly will the door yield to his thrust.

'. . . I was interrupted for three weeks,' Flaubert wrote, 'and had a hard task to put myself in train to work again. I have the peculiarity of a camel—I find it difficult to stop when once I get started, and hard to start after I have been resting.' [14]

We are capable of doing much more than we suppose.

What the novelist hopes for is a 'stream of composition,' in James's phrase, down which he can paddle from source to mouth, with no intervals but the nightly camp and fire. He welcomes white water now and again, or the portage round the falls. He has chosen the stream, and learns it well. He has faith in its direction, and a silent, exultant pride in the skill that brings him past the rapids and the roaring chutes.

27 the blank period

There are certain days, however, on which no word will follow another, and the imagination darkens like an empty screen. Such days are not frequent, but they usually come in twos and threes. They are probably a signal that the imagination has exhausted itself for the time and must be refreshed by rest and change.

Once the novelist has made sure that he is faced with one of these blank periods, and not merely an

unusually difficult resistance, he should give himself an undeclared holiday. It is nearly always
useless to fight such periods. The effort is out of all
proportion to the work done; and this work is usually so flat that it must be rewritten later.

So the novelist should take himself by the hand and
go blinking out into the world. He may not *want* a
holiday. He may be so completely caught up in the
book that he resents the necessity of breaking off
work. He may fret and grumble, or allow himself to
become a little panicked at the idea that he has
gone cold on the book, or even that he may not be
able to write for a long time again. Unless there are
other and tremendously more serious factors involved, this is nonsense, and he knows it. But he is
in a state of nonsense.

He feels bleary and miserable in the unaccustomed
early sunlight. He wanders into the park and en-
vies the ducks, who do not write books. The gold
eye of the panther in the menagerie, pacing off his
thousand miles a day, stares at him with a mindless
and unutterable ferocity. Even the smart women,
passing so briskly, hardly glance at him. He is obviously a man who has no business in a world where
everyone else is too busy to live.

He wishes he had money enough to go away for a
while, and discovers that he does not really wish it.
All he needs is to get back to the book. He is like a
shirt hung on a line between two worlds.

The next day is no better. But in a day or so more he sits down to work again; and the paragraph he has rewritten until the words have no meaning stirs and breathes. He writes another, and stares at it in wonder and relief. He has begun again.

28 the controlled relaxation

Whether he likes it or not, the novelist at work had better find means of relaxing. Curiously enough, he may *not* like it. He may be so caught up in the onset of his book that he begrudges every hour away from it. Moreover, the sooner it is done, the sooner he will have the elephant off his back.

Or he may be a congenital dawdler who clings to every diversion that promises to relieve him for a moment from the tension of writing. He may even combine both these feelings: the impulse to get done with the thing, and the impulse to get away from it.

In any case, the problem is the same. He needs to get what is enough relaxation, for him, but not too much; and it should be of the right kind. Every shading of the psyche or the soma will reveal itself in writing, though often in rather indirect ways. This is quite as true of muscle tone as it is of a psychic depression caused by illness.

The professional, one who is thoroughly aware of his own disabilities and tonic variations, will indeed almost unconsciously correct and compensate for these variations. He may write a passage which gives the effect of great buoyancy while he himself is suffering from the most acute unhappiness.

Here we may glimpse the secret heroisms of literature; and perhaps it is as well that they should remain secret. There is, of course, no one-to-one ratio in such matters. The relation is infinitely complex and tortuous. Great unhappiness may light a fire of noble words. Even a petty personal emotion —anger at the grocery man, who has refused credit —may be convertible, like fuel or other versatile energy, into a dozen apparently unrelated uses in writing. Wrath against the grocery man may, ridiculously enough, become passion in a love scene. The psychological series that makes possible this conversion of emotional energy is, of course, far more intricate than our description would suggest. Perhaps it is only one more means of access to the energies of the unconscious. If these energies, as in the case of the grocery man, are not converted, they may spoil a day's work.

But we are concerned here with the fact that man, even the novelist, is an organism that requires frequent and various kinds of activity. He will suffer from disuse of function. The novelist does not need an athlete's pitch of muscle tone. It might make him dull-witted in *his* work, though it does not necessarily make the athlete dull. What the novelist requires, evidently, is a good deal more modest: a redressed balance of muscle tone, a release and reintegration of motor impulses. This wholeness is deeply related—and not merely by analogy—to the integration of personality.

The kind of relaxation the novelist needs will depend on his temperament and body type, plus his social and esthetic tastes. A powerful Melville may find his balance in chopping wood; and the weight of the shoulder muscles, as it were, can be felt in his prose. A Henry James may take long walks about the streets of London. A Hemingway may troll for swordfish, a Faulkner breed mules, or a Dos Passos exercise the nice kinesthetic reflexes involved in handling a small boat under sail. But whether the novelist prefers table tennis or absinthe-drinking, his relaxation while he is at work on a book should be regular and varied enough to keep him in the best condition for his work.

Reading, except for reference reading or the invisible prose of newspapers and popular magazines, may have a bad effect, especially on the younger writer, who is trying to form and hold a style of his own. The better the work read—*Moby Dick* or the Bible or *Sevastopol*—the more disturbance it is likely to cause. This appears to be primarily a dis-

turbance of the rhythmic sense. It may even beget
echoes; and echoes are as uncomfortable in a stretch
of otherwise coherent prose as they would be in a
haunted house.

29 revision and rewriting

To *revise* is literally to look back, to *revisit*. In any
case, it is a looking, and the first business of the
novelist in revision is to look hard. He will not see
what he does not look at; and it is essential that he
should see as much as he can, and as finely as he
can.

Rewriting may be said to differ from revision in
that (A) it is a much fuller operation—not minor
alteration, in a clause or sentence, but whole paragraphs and pages redone; (B) it involves a change
in conception, or an attempt to bring the work
closer to the original conception.

We may also include here such functions as cutting,
recasting, the shifting of sections from one place to
another, expanding and contracting. All these,
except the last two, are patchwork and makeshifts.
They attempt to correct, by drastic means, what was
badly written in the first place. In a well-organized
book, all cutting, no matter how skilfully done,
leaves a scar. Like recasting and the shifting of
parts, it tends to disturb the delicate internal balance of a book in ways that not even the most experienced novelist or editor can wholly anticipate.

In good fiction, moreover, above and beyond all planned effects, there is a kind of organic or molecular flow, nonlogical in character, and derived from the spontaneous associative powers of the imagination. Necessarily arbitrary in detail, but arbitrary only within the given terms of the book, it is like a new river finding its way through a known landscape. This nonlogical logic may defy the most exquisite critical analysis. Even very skilful cutting or recasting may break it up and divert it in unforeseen ways. Often the novelist himself is unaware of this process in his work; but a dim sense of it may be at the root of his apparently unreasonable resistance to changes.

There may be exceptions—every novel tends to create its own conditions and precedents—but in general these remarks apply only to work of a professional character. In a loosely written book, such expedients as cutting and recasting may be unavoidable, if there is no time for a full rewriting, and no assurance that the author has enough technical skill (there *are* other kinds of skill in a novel) to make a second version more successful than the first. If the novel is intended to be purely commercial, the problem becomes less difficult. An accomplished editor, working with the author, can trim, shuffle and piece the book into a simulacrum as lively and quick-moving as the mechanical rabbit at a dog track.

Rewriting should precede revision. The rewritten passages will need to be scrutinized with the rest.

To *rewrite* is literally to *write again*. It is an axiom of the craft, having few exceptions, that good books are not written but rewritten. (This page has been reworked seven times.) Rewriting is called for when (A) the author regards a passage, for whatever reason, as unsatisfactory; (B) he feels that he can improve a passage already more or less competently handled; (C) he wishes to alter a passage in the light of a fresh conception. Flaubert might spend all day going over and over a sentence. Balzac rewrote incessantly, until even his proofs were smothered with changes. Howard P. Vincent [46] and Leon Howard have presented evidence to show that Melville rewrote *Moby Dick* entirely, out of a boundless new vision of it, after he had completed the book once as a simple 'whaling story.' Such examples might be multiplied into hundreds.

Some novelists prefer to rewrite each page until they are satisfied that it is the best they can do. Others may rework the book as a whole three or four times. Each method has its advantages. The method should suit the man; only the results count. But the central principle of all rewriting is that each change should bring the text a little nearer to the feeling-vision of the novelist, the precise sense of what he is trying to convey—a little nearer in fidelity, in realization, in acuteness, in eloquence, in distinct projection. This feeling-vision is the touchstone to which every effect must be referred.

Revision is a matter of taking endless pains. It calls for the patience of a mule and the concentration of a bank examiner going over a set of suspected ledgers. It is a rather narrow, predominantly intellectual function of the critical sense—an affair of taste, judgment, scrupulous observation, an acute ear for tone. But it must be regarded chiefly as applied knowledge of what are called, in education, 'tool subjects': spelling, word definitions, usage, systems of punctuation, syntax (formal syntax, and the 'ear' syntax of dialect or other speech), right down to such minor problems as tautology, pleonasm, pregnant construction, zeugma and the rest.

Some novelists prefer to revise in two operations: once over for the sense, and once for technical minutiae. These operations do seem to call for contrary types of attention. The first is analytic, the second a close scanning.

If the novelist will make an invariable habit of getting things straight in the first place—that is, if he will consult his dictionary or other reference when he first sets down a word or construction—he should have very little trouble with revision.

In rewriting or revision, the novelist should listen for the critical voice. Sometimes it says no boldly, and sometimes it is only a faint grumble of disapproval. The novelist who intends to publish nothing but his best work will never disregard this voice. The faintest doubt should be enough to provoke action in reexamining and rewriting the suspect point.

It is the gravest of critical errors, and arrogant condescension besides, to assume that the reader will be less perceptive than we are. He may, in the analysis of small technical events; but the failure of *effect* will not be lost on him.

A good, safe rule, in writing as in other kinds of living, is to take it for granted that our audience may be at least as perceptive as we are. As a matter of statistical chance, this is almost certain to be true in at least a few cases; and a few cases are enough.

It is almost certain *not* to be true, in regard to a particular novel, for the whole body of readers. This is the governing axiom of the popular writer.

In an ideal world, no novelist would attempt a thoroughgoing revision or rewriting until six months or so after he had finished the book. While he is working, and for some time afterward, his imaginative conception and the actual novel produced are so interactive that he is to some extent incapable of exercising objective judgment. Moreover, both conception and physical novel are deeply involved with his ego, which is by now rather abnormally sensitive to touch.

So far as he can, the novelist will discount his ego involvement as so much incidental nonsense, an occupational liability like any other. But he is faced with immediate decisions. The manuscript is going to the printer. The publisher and the editor both think that it should be cut here and slightly expanded there. They have reasons. The novelist must decide. He goes back over his outline and the work that derived from it. If he is a sensible man—or as sensible as a writer can be—he knows only too well that he may have been wrong in some calculation or proportion. He knows too that while he is still emotionally involved with a work, each paragraph may have an excessive—even an absurdly sacred—value to him.

But all this, he feels, is beside the point. The integrity of the work is his first concern. And since he respects the judgment of his publisher and editor, he feels that it is theirs too. Moreover, he is quite conscious that his own judgment is, for the time being, compromised.

Another man, or even the novelist himself, in some parallel situation, would not hesitate. He would accept the opinion of qualified people and be grateful for it. This may be the novelist's best course too, if he is not a thorough professional; or if his work-

ing methods tend to be somewhat vague and hap-
hazard; or if, after discussion, he is convinced that
changes should be made.

But in the end he should accept only the judgment
that he himself has formed, and for an obvious reason: only he is, or should be, an expert in his book.
He is not dealing merely with his judgment at the
moment. He is considering the progressive effects
of his judgment continuously exercised over a year,
or two, or three, in conception, planning, the choice
of means and methods, and in each day's work. His
judgment at the moment is relatively untrustworthy;
but this other, cumulative judgment tested through
the whole period of planning and writing is not.
Even this may turn out to be mistaken at certain
points. But it is all he has to go on.

30 the application and relaxation of pressures

The conscious control of pressure is perhaps a little
difficult to grasp as an idea, but simple enough in
practice.

At bottom, it is an aspect of 'qualitative progression.' It is one of the means of applying stress as 'the
qualitative factor in emphasis.'

We may assume that the novelist will write each
section of his book as firmly and thoroughly as he

can. He will bring all his resources to bear on it. Thus, if the matter were entirely logical, he would place a more or less equal pressure on *every* section, and the system of pressures would be determined by the relative saliency of the material in each case.

In practice, we know that this is not so—or only in random and highly qualified phases. It is what may be called a romantic fallacy, common enough in writers of first novels. Just as each section will suggest its own gradation of tone, so a sensitive novelist will catch its intimation of the degree of pressure it requires. Not every section can *bear* an equal pressure, or the same *kind* of pressure. Thus strong emphasis on a casual walk in the park, unless this emphasis is necessary for other reasons, may produce an unpleasant and irrelevant tension. It may also cause the reader to expect some portentous development not fulfilled in the event.

The Ambassadors provides, among many other examples, a fine piece of good management in this respect. This is the scene in which Strether leaves Paris for a day's wandering in the French countryside. It is relaxed and genial with a freshness of leaves in the sun, it gives us one more demonstration of his sensitive consciousness, and it leads sharply into the tension of the scene on the riverbank, where Strether discovers young Chad and Madame de Vionnet in circumstances that clearly indicate their sexual intimacy. The whole thing is a little triumph of 'qualitative progression' and a lesson in the deployment of pressures.

We may assume, then, that pressures *can* be controlled, and that their uses will be largely determined by the novelist's sense of what the scene will *bear* and what it *demands*. Certain scenes, of conflict or climax, will challenge his whole personality like a physical event in his own life. If he winces away from them, his effect by that much will fall short. If he does not, they will call out his deepest vitality, the most anguished reach of his courage, the fullest resource of his craft, his sensibility, his imagination—and not least, the weight of his conscious 'will.'

Just as he will respond to other scenes with his gentlest tactility, so he must focus all his powers, consciously, in the attack on his big scenes, much as an actor would. He must *drive* harder—without driving so hard that he discommodes himself. He must throw his full weight, timed and accurate, like a blocker in football.

31 the finish line

The last fifty-odd pages—the climax of the book, and its ending—are also the climax of the writer's effort. Even in a short novel, this effort may be intense. For a long one, in which all the lines of development must be brought together and exploded into an ultimate effect, the novelist throws in his last reserves of vitality—more than he had, or knew that he had. Like a runner in his final gasping sprint for the tape, the greatest effort is demanded of him when he has least left to give. No one paces him. Hollow-chested, he runs against phantoms; and only he will know, perhaps, whether he has given the last stroke of effort, or a little less.

There is some danger, indeed, that he may try *too* hard. A novelist coming up to the end of a long work may be in a condition approaching the hysterical. The very integrity of his personality is threatened. His state resembles the first full onset of love in a passionate sensibility. He is focused on the work as the lover concentrates on a woman; and the very exclusiveness of focus may distort his general vision. Discrimination leaves him; judgment falls off; he is capable of acting on powerful and arbitrary impulse.

Thus any extra degree of conscious effort may be unwise at this point. Pushed a little too far, the effect is likely to be hysterical. We may find examples of such effects, here and there, in the novels of George Meredith; in the later work of Thomas Wolfe; and in the ending of Steinbeck's *The Grapes of Wrath*.

'Would that a man could do something and then say—It is finished,' Melville wrote to Hawthorne.

'. . . But live and push—tho' we put one leg before
forward ten miles—its no reason the other must lag
behind—no, *that* must again distance the other—
& so we go till we get the cramp and die.' [46]

32 the reaction

When the novelist finishes a long book, or any book
that calls for an intense exhaustion of effort, the
immediate reaction is likely to be severe. Many
things are happening to him at once.

First, he is nervously exhausted, like any man who
has finished a long, hard job. The nature of his job
demanded the greatest stress at the end, a stress at
once acute and cumulative, so that the backlash of
nervous tension, suddenly released, tends to be
drastic in effect. This is accompanied, often enough,
by an emotional sensitivity so awakened and in-
flamed that it has the irritability of raw tissue.

'Sometimes,' said Balzac, 'it seems to me as if my
brain were on fire and as if I were fated to die on the
ruins of my mind.' [53]

Moreover, the novelist is by now one blocked charge
of accumulated motor impulses: (A) those impulses
naturally inhibited by the fact that he has been
sitting in a chair most of the time for a year or two;
and (B) the other thousands of what may be called
rudimentary motor impulses he has absorbed in

creating the experiences of his characters. Much of the energy in these latter impulses will, of course, be discharged in the book; but it is likely that they retain enough of their primitive organic character to behave like minor thwarted drives in the novelist himself.

Too, he will be uncomfortablely aware of the effects of related psysiological changes. He has been getting very little exercise. The more or less continuous nervous excitement of his work has released unusual amounts of adrenalin and blood sugar into the bloodstream, slowed down the activities of his alimentary canal, and contracted the round muscles of his intestines into so many steel bands. He is in the grip of the writer's old bête noire: a malfunctioning of the digestive tract at one point or another.

There are deeper, psychic issues involved. He has been straddling two overlapped worlds: the world of the book, and the actual world. He will be conscious of a kind of minor, forced schizoidism. This partial split or ambivalence will be uncomfortable, even painful, to the novelist not constitutionally inclined to it. It will make itself felt chiefly in the transitions from one major orientation to the other —the book to the world, or the world to the book. It may even account for the barking manners of writers disturbed at their work, an almost universal trait—though this can be, as is, explained on simpler grounds by the persons who are barked at.

The ambivalence we have noted may also disturb the major integration of the novelist's personality. He differs from other writers, poets or short-story writers, in the duration required for each work. Thus the strain on his personality is exercised over a longer period, and the recovery slower. Vincent observes that when Melville wrote *Pierre*, a year or so after he had finished *Moby Dick*, the signs of disintegrated personality were apparent, and strikingly in contrast with the vigorous wholeness of the earlier book. [46] Evidently Melville had not fully recovered from the strain of his greater work — though of course we must presume the intervention of other factors too.

'It was a work on which he had been engaged for several years — hence its completion likewise required of him some large measure of reidentification.' [4]

We may note a further possibility. The writing of a novel goes on so long that the novelist may have time to make a new, though perhaps partial, reintegration of personality which involves him in the book itself. We have a ready analogy here — Balzac's parallel between the book and the baby. Just as the mother, in pregnancy, makes a new integration with the child she is to bear, focusing her wishes and hopes on it, so the novelist may weave his functional personality into the evolving tissue of his book.

At first glance, we are perhaps a little inclined to scout this notion, or to regard it as overwrought, even ridiculous. The novelist, to begin with, is in this case the wrong sex. But are the sexes quite so well differentiated as that? Is it not far more likely that the maternal impulse and the paternal are aspects of a single human impulse, bisexual in character, and that this may be projected in the types of activity Koestler calls 'self-transcendence'? We observe that this is so in ordinary life; and there is much evidence to indicate that it may be so in the arts too.

In any case, the novelist has finished his book. At a certain moment—almost without warning, as he feels—it is over. He is tumbled out into the light of day, returned to the single world of the actual. He has a momentary overwhelming sense of thankfulness and relief. The elephant is off his back. He is free again. But this instant is succeeded at once by a feeling of vague loss, and a painful shaking newness in the bright world he has returned to. As one novelist has said, he is 'like a man coming up from the bottom of a well.'

Far down in him glows a single warm coal of pride. He has done it. But he is dismayed by the disorganization and inadequacy he feels now in himself, a new and surprising inadequacy that comes hard on the heels of his sense of powerful competence in driving through the last pages of the novel. He takes a look at the manuscript again, ostensibly to reassure himself that it came out well. What he is really looking for is his lost confidence. He feels unable to deal with the restored, common world. He gathers his personality about him as if it were an old coat. He is like a beggar who has dreamed of commanding a great ship in the tropics and awakes to find himself huddled in the snow.

In this first flash of reaction, the novelist's behavior will sometimes reach the point of being a little abhorrent to sensible people. He may cry like a child, pick a savage fight with his wife, or carry her off to bed so unceremoniously that she thinks of demanding money from him. He will perhaps take a train without bothering to consult the timetable. He may sleep for a week or get drunk for a week.

This last means that he is trying to discharge his motor impulses and make a drastic reorganization of personality at one stroke. The tendency is sound but the method unwise. He needs time—time for recovery, for the compensating swings of readjustment, for a slow, warm bathing in the natural world. He has had strain enough. He needs a gentle, active, simple life.

33 the aftereffects

The aftereffects are, in general, a prolongation of and adjustment to the difficulties mentioned in the first reaction: nervous exhaustion, hyperirritability, psychic and gastrointestinal disturbances. All these are in the main typical enough, mere phases of re-adjustment, and the novelist need not take them too seriously. This is cold comfort to a man in the midst of them; but he should be reassured by the knowl-edge that his troubles are the troubles of every novelist born.

To these, however, must be added certain other possibilities. If the novelist has any inherent psy-chotic, psychoneurotic, psychosomatic, or other gob-bledegook weaknesses—and if he does not have them, he need only invent them—they will show up now. Unless they get out of hand completely, he must deal with them. That is part of his business. Is he not an adept in human character? Then let him show his skill at home. It is also part of his business that he should know himself well enough to be able to discount, in his work, the defects and aberrations of his own personality. As the psycho-analyst Reik points out (no doubt to the horror of his colleagues, who see the labor of years in dis-crediting introspection swept away at a touch), the best analysis is self-analysis. [37] The novelist must learn how to adjust *himself*. The least he should know, in this respect, is how far he can push him-self without going over the cliffs, and which cliffs are his particular dangers.

It may be, too, that he has been swimming in dark waters. 'And if thou gaze too long into an abyss,' said Nietzsche, paraphrasing the comedians, 'the abyss will gaze into thee.' A steady contemplation of grief, illness, cruelty, pain, loss, death, the evil and infirmities of the universe, undergone as emotional experience, and intensely realized—all this will do him no more good than it might the next man, except as a sad accretion of wisdom.

True, the novelist has resources, in this respect, not usually available to others. He maintains some 'esthetic detachment'—an elegant phrase for the distance between the eye and the object. He projects feeling in the essentialized processes of art rather than in the immediate personal relation. Moreover, his sensibility is trained to take up shock and react quickly. In matters of the emotions—professionally, at least—the artist is a foam-rubber man, at once absorptive and resilient.

But there are limits, and the novelist will cross them often enough. When he had finished *Moby Dick*, Melville wandered the streets like a dismasted ship hardly answerable to her holm. In 1869, the year he put the last words to *War and Peace*, Tolstoy went to bed one night in the town of Arzamas and underwent a terrifying experience afterwards referred to in his family as the 'Arzamas misery.'

Later he described what was probably this same experience in *Diary of a Madman*: 'I felt that I could not go to sleep. Why had I come here? Where am I

going? What and how am I escaping? I am trying
to escape something terrible, which I cannot escape.
I am always with myself and I am the tormentor. I
—that is it.—I am here. . . . I am the one who
has tired myself, who is unbearable, insufferable to
myself. I want to fall asleep, to forget myself. . . .
I went out into the hall, hoping that I should escape
my tormentor, but he followed me and obscured
everything. I was terrified. What kind of stupidity
is this? Why all this misery, what am I afraid of?
"Of me," inaudibly answered the voice of death.
"I am here!" ' [35]

This is the thing itself, *in excelsis:* the noble health
of the great book, and its paradoxical effects in the
torn personality of its author; the experience undergone in all its fullness by a man of genius, and his
full re-creation of it. Perhaps a psychologist would
suggest the pathological. Reik does, quite casually,
in regard to Tolstoy. But the pathological is a matter of definition. Any novelist will recognize one of
those terrifying lifts and plummets, those disor-
ganized yaws and veerings, which are the signals
of the personality violently readjusting itself—the
homeostasis of the psyche. Tolstoy had struck bottom. Less than four years later, he began *Anna
Karenina.*

We may perhaps afford one more piece of testimony.
'After fifteen years of constant toil,' Balzac wrote to
Madame de Hanska, 'I cannot longer sustain this

struggle. *Créer, toujours créer!* God created only
for six days and rested on the seventh.'

Now that he has reached the end of his book, the
novelist too may rest for a while, except for publishers, editors, printers, reviewers—and even, perhaps, readers and tax-collectors. Then the direction
is *da capo*—from the beginning again.

part three: the novelist

'In short, I pass my life gnawing my heart and my brain—that is the real truth about your friend.' [14]

1 general axioms

IT IS better not to be a novelist if you can help it, and if you can help it you are not a novelist.

A novelist is a specialist in the general.

The novelist at work is a cat watching a mouse. The mouse may be literature, or money, or both. But it is very hard to concentrate on a two-headed mouse.

All other mice—fame, power, the well-fed ego, a gay life, self-expression, the hope of immortality,

the wish to be loved or to please one's friends—
will probably turn out to be phantoms. Even if they
are not, they can be caught more conveniently in
some other trap.

Except for the wording of his contracts, a novelist
is not an 'author.' When you call him that, smile.

The novelist, like other people, requires a theory of
limits. But he needs to remember that the potentialities of his medium are virtually unlimited.

He is free to do almost anything—anything that
skill, sensibility, judgment, the cold courage of his
attack, and an unbreakable devotion to the task can
accomplish.

People who do not write novels tend to think that
people who do exaggerate the difficulty of the task.
No humane novelist would suggest that these others
find out for themselves.

'Now I am myself vain enough to cherish the hope
of bequeathing something to posterity; I see no
reason for resigning my right to that inventive
freedom which others enjoy; and, as I have no
truth to put on record, having lived a very hum-
drum life, I fall back on falsehood—but falsehood
of a more consistent variety; for I now make the only
true statement you are to expect—that I am a liar.
This confession is, I consider, a full defense against

all imputations. My subject is, then, what I have
neither seen, experienced, nor been told, what neither exists nor could conceivably do so. I humbly
solicit my readers' incredulity.' [32]

'When I am not writing I am thinking over my plans,
and when I am not writing or thinking I have proofs
to correct. That is what my life consists of.' [53]

'It is a happiness to a man to be able to amuse himself with writing,' said Brackenridge. 'For it is not
everyone that can play upon the violin, or the flute;
and the fingers must be employed some way.'

2 the personality

Now let us look at the genus *homo scriptor*.

He may be intensely methodical, like Flaubert, or
intensely disarranged, like Lawrence. He may live
like a newspaper reporter, as Stephen Crane did;
or like a retired industrialist, as some of our popular
writers do; or like an amateur redeemer, as Tolstoy
did toward the end; or like a man of means and a
diner-out, as Henry James did.

He may be an unresting traveler, like Gautier or
Stevenson or Dos Passos; or, like Jane Austen, he
may hardly wander from his home earth.

Between one experienced novelist and another, the
difference in the degree of awareness as to who he

is, what he is doing, and how he does it is literally astonishing. This, almost in itself, is enough to account for the furious disagreements among writers in regard to theory and method.

But there is a larger factor, perhaps the basic one. Novelists, like other people, come in all the known personality types—plus perhaps a few not yet thoroughly explored. They show the diversities of these types, intensely particularized in the individual. Their life experience will be equally diverse; and by the very nature of their profession, this experience will tend to be still further individuated, though they may make conscious and more or less successful efforts toward socializing it.

This has two aspects. The first is that a working novelist spends a great deal of his time alone—far more than most men ever do. The second is that, like an actor's, his personality—by which we mean his whole psychophysical equipment—is his chief stock in trade. It is also, like the actor's, the controlled instrument by means of which he creates his effects. We may easily lose sight of this close analogy between the actor's and the novelist's arts. One works in a public medium, the other in a private one. The actor moves in empathic relation with an audience; the novelist must imagine his audience—and all too often finds out later that it *was* imaginary. But we may observe how the novelist and the actor came together in such writers as Charles

Dickens and Mark Twain. These men and others, in public readings from their books, became at once the actor and the traditional oral storyteller.

We may also remark that the novelist will have a social personality which does not usually or wholly correspond to his private and professional one. In this he does not differ very much from other men; but for various reasons, the effect will be more salient in his case. For him, as for most men, his work in the center of his life. But, more than for most men, this center is inside him. His office is in the cortex and epencephalon and thalamencephalon, in the nerves and muscles and viscera, in the imagination and the intellect. Thus, when he talks about his work, he must—even more than most men—talk about himself. This earns him the name of being an egocentric. For such reasons and others, many sensitive writers may prefer not to talk about their work at all, or pass it off flippantly. But that is only the other side of the medal.

Thus novelists may tend to show certain traits in common. They share a number of liabilities: aloneness and its concomitant shyness or sociability, like that of a miner down from the hills; more day-to-day financial insecurity than many men know; the habit of personal initiative, and the associated habit of making a thousand completely independent decisions for their books and their characters, often and necessarily on a plane removed from the level of ordinary ethics. This is not meant to suggest that a novelist is likely to steal anyone's wallet. He is far less likely than most men. Almost certainly, at one time or another, he has got used to a kind of chronic insecurity that would drive the average employed man to the edge of panic.

The novelist comes to regard such things as standard occupational risks. He will tend to be a little too careless about money, or a little too careful. He will also perhaps show a certain brusqueness, or a parrying humor, or a smooth and courteous evasiveness. These are all marks of the same necessity. He has become skilled at guarding his personality, because his personality is his work, and his work is his life. Like the throwing arm of a baseball pitcher, it is the asset that signs his contracts for him. He prefers to risk it in use. But he is quite likely to get tired of this and commit indiscretions a little more reckless than other people's. He knows very well that all growth is risk. Moreover, the habits associated with writing, and his long absorption in a book, will necessarily make him seem a little unsociable at times even to his most indulgent friends. He will need to refuse too many invitations; and he must have some means of discounting this if he can.

'What a charming profession!' said Flaubert. 'It is like whipping cream when one would like to be rolling marbles.' [14]

Will is a somewhat discredited term among the psychologists. What shall we call it then—the 'will' of the novelist? An unconscious drive reinforced by intense conscious volition? Zweig speaks of 'the unbending, unshakable will power of Honoré de Balzac which, now that Napoleon was broken, had not its match in Europe.' We may suspect that there was something a little obsessional about the drive of the Balzacian 'will.' But it was, at most, only an exaggeration, a supreme archetype, of the crushing pressure every novelist must fasten on himself if he intends to write his book, and the book after that, and the book after that.

3 the sensibility

'. . . the kind and degree of the novelist's prime sensibility, which is the soil out of which his subject springs. The quality and capacity of that soil, its ability to "grow" with due freshness and straightness any vision of life, represents, strongly or weakly, the projected morality.' [26]

The typical sensibility of the novelist, with its collateral verbal facility, will often appear in early youth and become pronounced, like that of other artists, in a stormy adolescence.

Burke suggests that 'every one has the artist's temper as an adolescent'; and this gives us, in some degree, a common ground of reference.

He speaks of Flaubert's adolescence: 'the cult of the illicit,' the cynical analysis, the yearning for a central identity, the exuberance. 'I want a mass of fun,' said young Flaubert, 'of riot, of violent activity, the whole thing dumped *pêle-mêle*, in a heap, without order, without style [sic] . . .'

He wanted to get away, to the Ganges, to 'the noise of the water in the rushes, to the cooing of birds perched on the yellow trees.' He believed that he had a kinship with animals, the diseased, the psychotic. 'I attract animals and the insane,' he wrote.

The signs are typical enough—the efflorescence of the senses, the urgent and diffuse emotion. We feel the disorder of impulses not yet concentrated on an object: on a girl, an adventure, or a book. When the object appears, it will act as a nucleus for the crystallization of sensibility, like that branch encrusted with glittering salt which Stendhal used as an emblem of the crystallization of love.

This is the key to the uses of sensibility: that it should have an object. This object becomes at once a core, a principle of accretion, and a selective agent. The novel is such an object, and an object, moreover, so various and variously demanding that it will provide a core for every aspect of the data of sensibility.

How is this data gathered? In effect, we may say that it gathers itself, though the novelist must some-

times make a conscious effort to grasp it. It is a
function of his drives, his interests, the inflection
of his personality. It is the way he lives. He comes
to know about people because he is interested in
people. Thus the question as to whether he should
train himself as a highly conscious observer calls
for many qualifications. It may be a matter of particular occasions, or of rather specialized data. He
may, for example, find it necessary to observe the
phases of an industrial process. Or he may feel the
broader need of strengthening his observation in
some field in which he considers it deficient.

But in general, we may say that a cultivated literal
awareness will perhaps cause us to miss more than
we catch. Sensibility is of many kinds, and involves
the whole personality, in what may be called its
cluster of 'natural' relations. Thus, in any social
situation, the habit of conscious literal observation
may prevent us from catching the finer and less
tangible intimations of persons and things. Such
awareness is aggressive, and will perhaps inhibit
a more sensitive receptiveness. Moreover, since it
is an arbitrary distortion of our personality, it may
tend to create a consequent distortion in the field
of observation. A detective comes to see things in
certain ways, and in those ways only.

The chief disadvantage of a too literal awareness,
perhaps, is that its very particularity breaks up the
wholeness of our perceptions—that wholeness

which is composed of many aspects in a specific and
unique relation to each other. But we must not appear to rule out the uses of a sharp awareness in the
novelist. Its immense serviceability is not to be discounted. Neither should we regard a passive receptiveness as the largest aspect of sensibility. Human beings are not mere protoplasm. For every
novelist, the problem becomes a matter of integrat-
ing the most favorable measure and degree of
awareness, for him, in the most harmonious relation
with his whole sensibility.

4 the education of a novelist

There is a storyteller in every man, woman and
child, just as there is a musician, or a scientist, or a
philosopher. That is why people are willing to read
a story, or listen to music, or consider other people's
ideas. What makes the difference is the strong temperamental bent and the degree of cultivation.

We might assume that the natural force of his interests would push a writer or musician in the direction of his chief talent. Sometimes this is so,
sometimes not. All sorts of external factors may be
concerned in it, including the social. Every teacher
of writing has known students who seemed obviously cut out to be painters, but who were resolved, on the slightest grounds, to become writers
or break their necks in the attempt. And many

painters—John Marin and Marsden Hartley, among others—have shown verbal gifts so pronounced that they might have turned out to be professional writers if they had not chosen the better part.

At any age, the prospective writer may take a test. Aptitude tests are not decisive, but they will usually indicate his most promising directions. If he does not make a high verbal score, he would probably be unwise to attempt to write a novel. But this may not always be so. He may develop a limited but adequate verbal facility. Nor does the high verbal score, in itself, guarantee those other qualities necessary to the composition of a novel.

A little self-investigation will help to steer a writer away from what may be the wrong *kind* of writing, for him. If he is an 'introverted sensation type,' it is unlikely that he will do well with a novel about a bullish trader on the stock exchange. It is also unlikely, of course, that he would be interested in the first place.

A writer has his own effective means of externalizing the psyche: habitual introspection, and the act of writing itself. A reasonable estimate of the probabilities, balanced against his own self-knowledge, ought to give him his bearings.

Obviously, talents do not exclude each other. A writer may also be a painter, or a painter an architect. Moreover, the novel itself is broad and hospitable enough to enfold all sorts of compounded talents.

The wise novelist, like the wise man, will take all life, and all of his life, as a continuous education.

This education begins before he is aware of it, and goes on as long as he is sentient, often in ways that he is not conscious of. 'I believe that living is a skilled trade,' said Mercedes Miró in *The Bay of Silence* [33]. How much more skilled, then, must be a trade that sets out to organize living into a coherent and meaningful demonstration in fiction?

Preferably before he is thirty, a novelist should have read everything worth bothering about, plus a good many things not particularly worth bothering about but nourishing to his imagination.

A diet confined to 'the best' will starve him off almost as quickly as a diet limited to 'the worst.' The development of relative taste and standards requires a certain familiarity with the items to be related. One novel is not bad because another is better. An insistence on nothing but 'the best' marks the insecurity of the cultural snob. At a certain point, a writer may be able to learn more from a good popular Western novel by Ernest Haycox than he would from Mann or Flaubert.

If this reading is to be any good to him, it must be largely an experience prior to writing. The novelist must do it early and have it well digested before he sets out on his own major writing. The problem of 'echoes' from other men's work is quite simply the problem of reading which has not been assimilated in the writer's imagination, plus perhaps a certain too-easy suggestibility which will later be outgrown.

The best method of learning the art and craft of the novel is to read what other novelists have written, plus what good critics have said about it. The making of literature is a culture trait, a tradition, an art, and a way of formulating experience. As each child recapitulates the experience of his culture, so the incipient novelist needs to live through the historic experience of literature. Even new departures require a point of departure. The novelist may never wish to write as Lyeskov or Peacock wrote; but unless he knows *how* they wrote, he will not know how he is writing.

In the beginning, he will read for pleasure, and if he is lucky this pleasure will never be entirely lost, even though he may be condemned to the galleys of book-reviewing. But the quality of his pleasure will change. Gradually he will become more critical, he will begin to reject certain aspects of a book and welcome others, he will set up an order of values. Finally, in the third stage, which may be concurrent with the second, he will read a novel largely in order to recreate the artist's intention and the successive procedures by means of which he worked to carry it out. That is, the novelist will find pleasure in the formal process for its own sake.

It is this last stage that Henry James meant when he made his plea 'for Criticism, for Discrimination, for Appreciation on other than infantile lines—as against the so almost universal Anglo-Saxon absence of these things; which tends so, in our general trade, it seems to me, to break the heart. . . .'

The second-best method of learning to write a novel, which should accompany the first, is to find a good instructor. It has often been said that writing cannot be taught. This is a mysterious dogma the sense of which, if any, may escape even the most determined reflection. Has anyone ever argued that music or painting could not be taught? Anything can be taught, if the teacher is competent and the student apt and willing. The teacher may be a dead technician, such as Henry James, or a living one, such as Ralph Bates. In any event, he will have experienced a profound and painful dedication to his art; and he will feel the guildsman's pride in handing it on faithfully and well.

It is curious that a student musician will spend years learning the technical refinements of his art; that a student architect may devote whole terms to drawing lintels and courses before he is allowed to attempt the simplest plan; but that a student

novelist will feel himself obscurely bilked and
balked if he is not given the gist of his art, complete, in ten shining axioms.

Can an instructor who is not a novelist teach novel-
writing? It is hard to see why not, though we may
perhaps find it difficult to imagine a teacher of
music who is not in some sense a musician, or a
teacher of painting who does not paint. The non-
professional teacher of the novel may not do it quite
so well as a good practicing technician who is able
to communicate what he knows—or so badly as a
novelist who is cloudy about method and rather
inarticulate in formulating it.

The teacher can make certain principles and methods *available* to the writer. After that, the complex
and indirect metabolism of each writer will reject
such data or convert it, by mysterious solutions, to
his own use.

Both the good teacher and the good student should
know that authority is not only irrelevant but harmful. If a teacher asserts this authority, he is *per se* a
bad teacher. The habit of independence—heart,
mind, and viscera—is more essential to the novelist
than the habit of good syntax. Any effective authority implies submission, and submission is a kind
of dependence. Even a mild habit of dependence
may be crippling in an art that demands the continuous exercise of the freest volition. It is the first

business of the teacher to see that this volition is cultivated, even at the cost of a mishandled scene or a bungled chapter.

The novelist, even the student novelist, who accepts borrowed authority will have none in his work. He must test every principle for himself.

Like a professional beauty, the novelist needs to devote himself to the perpetual cultivation of his good points and the compensation of his defects. Is he good at catching the tone of a group of charac- ters? Then let him become better yet. Has he a bad ear for the shadings of speech? Then let him listen harder. Does he notice women's clothes but ignore the trees and the sky? Then let him put his observation of women on short commons and learn to inspect the volumes of the cumulus or the leaves of the magnolia.

The larger part of a novelist's education will always be the education of his senses and his sensibility, the habit of free association, the ability to deduct meanings from the interplay of personalities or to select patterns out of a multitudinous experience. In these matters, the ways of the imagination are difficult to estimate. Long after the event, it may present us with some detail or circumstance we had never been conscious of observing—a detail that illuminates the whole.

A novelist requires the broadest possible field of reference: poetry, the warm sky, travel, Chateaubriand's ideas, the look of an overdrive assembly, and the infinite changeability of persons. Nor does he stand in much peril of diffusion. Each of his novels, as he comes to it, will provide the necessary and specific focus. The more he has gathered, the more he will have to choose from. And choice—of detail, of action, of emotion, of persons—is at the heart of his craft.

5 the novelist as a writer

A novelist is part of a writer, and a writer is part of a man—or the whole man, as Flaubert believed.

Aside from his novelist phase, he may be a writer of verse, or short stories, or motion-picture scripts. Or he may be a factual writer working on antibiotics or ethnological reports. All these will tend to modify his field of vision and his angle of awareness. All these, if he can assimilate them, will nourish his faculty as a novelist.

Newspaper reporting, or any considerable amount of writing against a deadline, may be bad for the novelist. Such work enforces a drastic modification of his field of perception; and this modification, like the accompanying verbal method, will tend to become a powerful habit. A good novelist does not usually make a good reporter, or vice versa.

The writing of advertising copy, with its pointed
locutions and skeletal syntax, will perhaps have an
even more unfortunate effect.

But in the matter of occasional work, only bad writing—that is, writing not good of its kind, or not the
best the writer can do in that kind—is likely to be
bad for the novelist.

If he finds that his basic habit of perception is
changing, that he is becoming more and more of an
antibiotics researcher and less and less of a novelist,
then he must choose.

The novel is a jealous mistress.

6 alternative or concurrent occupations

'If I take a job I am lost,' the young Balzac wrote.
'I should become a clerk, a machine, a circus horse
with prescribed hours for doing my thirty or forty
laps in the ring, drinking, eating, and sleeping.'
[53]

But Stendhal said that if he had known about a
writer's life when he was young, he would have
studied to be 'an extractor of teeth, or a lawyer. . . .'

By and large, these are the classic attitudes of the
novelist in youth and the mature novelist respec-

tively. They make an accurate epitome of his dilemma.

A novelist should take the trouble to be born with a good income. Tolstoy, Proust and James, among others, displayed this admirable forethought. The results are evident in the quality—and more particularly, in the volume—of their production. They had time to work.

Failing that, the novelist should arrange to be a girl child. She can marry early, lock the children in the broom closet, and write her books. This may be bad for the children, but they will probably turn out no worse than most writers' children do. Any woman who has enough organizing ability to write a good novel should be able to condense the housework into two hours of the morning. Then she is free.

There are other advantages. She will have no wife to resent her presence in the zamindary all day, a wife who is alternately overanxious about her husband's welfare and hardly able to conceal her sense of superiority in the face of his ridiculous and stubborn habits. Doing nothing—which is what a novelist appears to be doing when he is planning and adding and subtracting and evoking—is considered somewhat less reprehensible in a woman than in a man.

If the incipient novelist has been careless enough to be born a male without an income, he is in trouble.

He may regard the traditional straits of writers as so much careless nonsense and bad judgment. He may plan a career and an income for himself as carefully and modestly as a young man just entering the banking business. More than that, he may actually walk the line he has laid down. He may, in short, try to be as reasonable as he likes. The unreasonable circumstances will find him out.

Writing novels is not a career, or a profession, or even a trade. It is a gambling game. The player's chances are somewhat less favorable than if he were betting on the horses, though the stakes are sometimes larger.

We may take it as axiomatic that the young man who sets out to write novels for a living is a wilful idiot.

He should remember that he has only himself to blame. No one asked him to be a novelist; and it may be that many people asked him not to. Society is not responsible for his misdemeanors, and will properly take no responsibility. Unless he has a regular job, he is not even eligible for social security benefits in the United States. He is, of course, required to pay income tax—if his upstart income should aspire so high.

Let us consider a little of the evidence. As long ago as 1800, Charles Brockden Brown, regarded as our earliest 'professional' novelist, said of writing that the most 'any American can look for, in his native country, is to be reimbursed his unavoidable expenses.' With a few exceptions, such as N. P. Willis, his words might have fitted any American writer until nearly the end of the nineteenth century.

'Dollars damm me,' said Melville. He meant that the lack of them did.

'I am very glad for your sake that you have studied a profession,' Dr. Ravenel said to young Captain Colbourne in *Miss Ravenel's Conversion*. 'A young man brought up in literary and scientific circles is subject to the temptation of concluding that it will be a fine thing to have no calling but letters. He is apt to think that he will make his living by his pen. Now that is all wrong; it is wrong because the pen is an uncertain means of existence; for no man should voluntarily place himself in the condition of living from hand to mouth.'

Until 1891, no copyright law gave American writers an equal footing with the Europeans. The American writer must be paid royalties or shares. Nothing — or a mere honorarium for proofs or first copies — need be paid to the European writer whose works were pirated. This may very well be a key fact in the history of our literature. By pinching off the growth of native works and flooding the American market with European ones, it helped to keep our outlook colonial. European authors whose books were pirated did not love us; and they mentioned this fact to the world. Robbers are not popular with the robbed. Nor did the American author—Cooper, for example—escape being pirated in Europe.

By the middle of the twentieth century, the financial prospects of the American novelist had so far improved, and the wildly mistaken prepossessions about them were so generally accepted as fact, that a young novelist might be forgiven for imagining that he had a good chance to make a living out of writing.

Let us see what his chances were. The figures we must deal with are certainly open to exception or dispute at many points. But they are perhaps the best available ones. We might select 1948, a year of almost unexampled American prosperity. In that year, the best estimate would indicate that there were some 9,000 so-called free-lance professional writers in the United States. We are concerned with these, not with employed writers, though the categories may overlap in a large number of cases. We shall consider only the gross income of free-lance writers from their self-employed work.

From this 9,000 let us select a group of 2,000 professionals who include most of the top-rank writing names in America — top-rank in respect to both prestige and earnings. In 1948, of these 2,000, some six out of nine earned less than $3,000 for that year, and the average gross income for the whole group might be generously estimated at $2,300. Since the sample comprised a number of very large incomes, we may assume that many of those at the lower end of the bracket fell far below the $2,300 average. But even this is munificent by the standards of the comparable professional artists' group, which averaged about $1,500 for the year.

Certain writers did earn a great deal of money, if we might trust the gross figures on the checks. The likeliest compilations suggested that perhaps forty to fifty American writers earned from $80,000 to $100,000 in 1948. There were some 130 authors in the $40,000 to $50,000 class; and some 300 more earned $8,000 to $30,000 — most of these at the lower end of the scale. A few more might be placed in the gaps between these typical brackets. The figures, of course, include income for writing from all sources — the larger part of it, perhaps, derived in many cases from the sale or lease of such 'subsidiary rights' as magazine publication and motion-picture rights.

Such figures may give us a false view of the situation. The book publisher's advance must be refunded out of earned royalties; and he will take from fifteen to fifty percent of the various 'subsidiary rights' sold or leased. Ten percent of all income received by the writer, in most cases, must go to his agent, who has usually earned it in a whirlwind of negotiations. The Federal and state governments will require a considerable share.

Thus we may conclude that, for the player who likes very long odds, writing has its merits as a gambling game that offers respectably high stakes. But how does the gambler live while he gambles? As a means of earning a living, writing must be ranked considerably below such trades as part-time plumbing and truckdriving.

In *The Writer's Book* [1], James A. Michener puts it bluntly and well. The prospective novelist, he says, should be reminded 'that it is hard to find a publisher, that when a novel is published it is hard to get it reviewed, that when a book is reviewed it is difficult to sell enough copies to make money, and that when one does actually make some money it is usually not enough to live on. Those are the facts.'

The basic dilemma of the novelist may be stated very simply. If he spends all his time writing novels, he will not usually make enough money to live on. Sooner or later, he must stop what he is doing and do something else to earn money. But even if he is qualified for some other trade or profession, and works at it, he will probably not be able to afford enough time or concentration to do his best work in

the novel. Let us assume that he does. He must still
live with a divided mind, work twice as hard as the
next man, and get only a part of what he considers
his 'own' work done.

Obviously no sensible man would have anything
to do with such an arrangement. We must conclude that the novelist is not sensible. We have seen
that the gambling odds are heavily against him, and
that he has very little chance of making a living at
writing. Unless he is a naive beginner, he must also
be aware that the social prestige is relatively small.
No matter how well-known he may become, any
motion-picture star will rank him. We cannot rule
out such factors entirely; but we must suppose that
the novelist is a man driven by a cultural rage so
intense that he will walk through walls in the effort
to get to his goal.

If he is not, if he regards writing as a hobby, he
may have a pleasant time and occasionally make a
little extra money for himself. Or again, if he thinks
of writing solely as a business, and accommodation
to the wishes of editors as his first duty, there is a
chance that he may do very well. The difficulty here
is that the same degree of skill, effort and intelligence, applied to some other business or profession,
would almost certainly bring in much larger re-
turns.

But for the professional novelist who happens to be
an artist, or who is otherwise unable to accommo-

date himself to commercial demands, the case is
clear. He must have some other trade, business or
profession. If he is wise or lucky, he will have
learned this early enough to get the training he
needs. But early or late, he must get it. He may become a customs inspector, like Melville; or a country editor, like Sherwood Anderson; or a breeder of
mules, like William Faulkner. He may become a
seaman, or a teacher, or an automobile mechanic.
But unless he has learned this lesson and applied it
thoroughly, his work and his life will suffer in ways
that he can hardly imagine.

The history of the professional novelist is the history of a man who lives on hope and eventually dies
of it.

7 the writing regimen

'He always observed extreme regularity in his work
each day. He yoked himself to it as an ox is yoked
to a cart, without waiting for that inspiration which
expectation renders fruitless, as he said. His energy
of will for all that concerned his art was prodigious,
and his patience was tireless. . . .' [6]

So much for Flaubert's method. He demanded
regularity, familiar conditions, a set task—the regimen of a clerk on his stool.

Other novelists find it possible to work anywhere,
or at any time: at home or on a visit, in a train or

aboard ship, on a bus or a mountainside. They are like women knitting.

Still others must work at night. Zweig writes of Balzac: 'It was only at night, when time was boundless and undivided, that continuity was possible, and in order to obtain this continuity of work he reversed the normal division of time and turned his night into day.' [53]

Novelists have favored certain cities as work places: Rome, Venice, Florence, Paris, London, New York, San Francisco, New Orleans. This has usually been explained on the ground of tradition and 'charm.' But there is perhaps more to it than that. When his day's work is finished, the novelist can walk out and lose himself in an instant. The energy and gaiety of the human swarm envelop him again. He is at once—in imagination, at least—delivered from his solitude. He is aware of a dense human medium which is not merely an agglomeration of people, as in Los Angeles, but which has its own cultural tone and depth. He may not know how valuable this is unless he has tried to work in such a city as Detroit, or in the sharp industrial cities of the American Southwest, where the practice of literature becomes an activity without social roots, hardly to be distinguished from hallucination.

Other novelists may prefer a house on the shore, or in the country, and find surf or crickets better medicine than the crowd.

But it is far more likely that the novelist will have as little to say about where he lives as most men do. Except for those desperate occasions when he risks everything to get a book done, he must live near his job, like other men.

The sense of place will be only one element in the nexus of his writing habits. He will have a favorite pen, a certain color of ink, paper of a special grade, an old typewriter as familiar to his hand as the razor he uses each morning.

He will make many more or less private discoveries, and apply them. He will note that there is a curious relation between temporary hunger and the release of the unconscious in writing. When Melville was working on *Moby Dick*, his wife wrote that he 'would sit at his desk all day not eating anything till four or five o'clock.' [46]

The novelist will remark that a little travel, or any slight change in routine, will sometimes have the same effect. He will observe that his best insights often come to him in the half-hour after he wakes up in the morning, or on waking from a short sleep at any time, or when he is too tired to sleep at night.

He will discover that making love and the euphoria of its aftermath freshen his perceptions and liberate the unconscious. Or that the tension of needing love, once broken, may have much the same result.

In a larger sense, he will be aware that any considerable change in metabolism, from a drinking party to convalescence after a serious illness, will tend to release a new stream of psychic energy in writing.

Here we may perceive a common organizing factor. Out of such elements as these each novelist constructs a nexus of work habits. This is his writing regimen. It may appear wholly eccentric to other people. But he has found out, by a thousand processes of trial-and-error, that it is the most efficient method for him—more efficient than any method a dozen time-study men could devise. A milkman who works at night is not considered odd, but a writer may be. Both do it for the same reason: they have found out that it is the best time to get the work done.

8 occupational disorders of the novelist

Sooner or later every novelist will develop occupational disorders, just as the cowhand develops bow legs, or the motion-picture executive a sense of Olympian betrayal.

These disabilities of the novelist are in general so familiar, and so evidently occupational in origin, that we need hardly do more than list them. Some of them have been considered elsewhere.

The Gastrointestinal Tract. Mérimée had a 'painful irritation' of the intestines. Was this what has come to be called 'colitis'? Dickens had hemorrhoid, or a fistula. James practised a digestive fad called 'Fletcherizing.' Conrad and Crane were 'dyspeptic.' The roll might be extended into hundreds. Significantly, it does not appear to include the cyclothyme physical types—Balzac, for example, or Melville.

Temporary Psychic Upsets Consequent on the Writing of a Book. We have cited the cases of Melville and Tolstoy, and discussed such presumable factors as a forced schizoidism, blocked motor impulses, a generalized tension, and some arrest of the digestive processes resembling that described by Cannon in conditions of fear, rage, etc.

We may suggest a somewhat different but related situation, in which the novel itself becomes a means of projecting and resolving psychic conflict. There is a particularly striking and well-documented example of this in Bernard DeVoto's *Mark Twain at Work.* Here, in a study of how Twain finally came to write *The Mysterious Stranger,* we may trace such an agonizing conflict through all its divagations from onset to resolution. We can admire the clarity of DeVoto's exegesis even if we do not wholly agree with his interpretation.

Since Lombroso, and perhaps earlier, it has been fashionable to suggest a significant community be-

tween the artist and the psychopath. Certainly as
many true psychopaths may be found among novelists as in any comparable group. Moreover, the
cases are plainer; all art is a kind of self-revelation,
though only in an infinitely qualified sense. It is
also, as we have seen, a technique for objectifying
psychic conflict, and so discharging it in a socially
meaningful way.

But if art were no more than this, we need hardly
trouble ourselves about it here. Thus, in the notion
that there is any usual or necessary connection between the practice of literature and the psycho-
pathic, we may suspect a certain naïveté in the
beholder's eye—a naïveté that writers themselves,
especially the romantics, have done much to en-
courage and compound.

Burke, once more, states the central point plainly.
Art, he writes, has been called a 'waking dream';
and 'today we understand it to mean art as a waking dream for the artist. . . . It is, rather, the
audience which dreams, while the artist oversees
the conditions which determine this dream.' [3]

We may go so far as to suggest that the typical disorders of the novelist *are* typical precisely because
they are *effects* of the occupational and environ-
mental stresses inseparable from his work and his
regimen. He does not usually *begin* that way. He
gets that way; and the measure of his competence,

the test of his validity and power as an artist, lie in the actions he has won, not in the small scars he has collected by the way.

9 the novelist as artist

'An artist is usually a damned liar,' said D. H. Lawrence, 'but his art, if it be art, will tell you the truth of his day.'

Why do we write novels instead of carving giant legends in the red sandstone buttes of Monument Valley?

In the anthropologist's sense, the production of literature is a culture trait like any other—*something people do in a particular culture at a particular time.*

Like other culture traits, it may be more or less fixed; ascendant or declining; relatively distinct, or symbiotic with other traits. It may command great social prestige, or almost none. In any event, it is a mere choice, arbitrary in the history of human cultures, more or less approved in ours.

Thus all attempts to justify, demean or rationalize the practice of literature are finally, though perhaps not immediately, irrelevant. These attempts, in themselves, are further manifestations of our culture. The cry of 'art for art's sake' is as meaningless as the cry of 'art for money's sake.' Literature is a function of its culture, or of certain of the many cultures we call 'human culture.' We hope to be paid for it, and paid well, because that too is one of the imperatives of our culture; but we beg the question if we attempt to think of it solely or primarily as a *means* of making money. Why literature then? Why not transportation, or the manufacture of metal alloys? To choose literature, as Balzac and many a writer since has learned, is indeed to take the long way round.

10 the novelist as a business man

Even the title of this section may cause a dim smile in any editorial office.

We should mention at once that we refer only to a possible and desirable situation. Occasionally, in matters of business, the novelist may be a snowy lamb, or he may hold out for more than he can reasonably hope to get. He may be a very offhand negotiator who is subsequently outraged—and not with himself—at discovering the clauses he has missed. Or he may be a man rendered literally desperate by the consciousness of debt and other obligations, a man who has focused his whole future on the prospects for this one book. But whatever else he may be, he is not always a business man who can strike a sharp and equitable bargain with a full knowledge of the conditions governing it.

Nor is the novelist entirely to blame. Even chrome-steel executives from the major industries have been known to blink once or twice on being introduced to the Alician world of book publishing. Some of its methods are uncomfortably rigid, others all too flexible. Moreover, the writer occupies an anomalous position in relation to it. He is neither inside the business, nor a customer. He resembles rather a subcontractor who supplies parts or rents patents to a larger industry.

In the matter of bargaining, the novelist is usually at a disadvantage. Very often he has got himself into a hole writing the book and needs money urgently. He likes the publisher who has offered to bring out the book; or he does not like the alternative of shopping around for another.

It is a hard business to learn from the outside. But willy-nilly, in one way or another, the novelist must pick up what he needs to know about it. This does *not* include the details of printers' contracts and the current paper quotations. It comprises, principally, these items: (A) an almost verbatim knowledge of the book contract, the fluidity of its clauses, and the effective meaning of each—more particularly, a thorough acquaintance with the implications of the 'subsidiary rights' clauses; (B) a clear notion of what a novelist of his standing may be able to ask for in the present state of the market; (C) some understanding of the etiquette of the editor's office;

and (D) a reasonable view of what he may expect in the way of sales promotion and advertising.

The novelist must find this information where he can. A detailed reading of *The Protection and Marketing of Literary Property* [50] will do him no harm. More experienced writers may be able to advise him. From first to last, he should consult the Authors Guild. Even if his agent negotiates his contracts for him, and does it very well, it is still necessary that he should learn the details of his own business. If it does nothing else, it will sharpen his knowledge of human character.

He owes this minimum sophistication to his publisher, who may become a little weary of explaining that it is hardly possible to get a book out in three weeks.

He owes it to himself and his fellow writers. Each time he signs an unwise contract, or fails to carry out the provisions of his contract, he depresses by so much the common credit of all writers.

11 the authors guild

If he is able to qualify, every novelist or prospective novelist should be a member of the Authors Guild of the Authors League of America.

Whether he is a member or not, the Authors Guild is engaged in promoting his interests. It can do better work, for him and for his fellow writers, if he is a member. The novelist should make no mistake about this. For the most part, if such work is not done by the guild, nobody will do it—or some individual writer must try to take it on his own shoulders, as Mark Twain did when he went before Congress to obtain copyright relief.

By the middle of the twentieth century, the league had become the parent body of a half-dozen trade guilds. It had its counterparts in many countries—in the French authors' society, the Canadian Authors' Association, and the English Incorporated Society of Authors, Playwrights, and Composers, founded in 1884 by Sir Walter Besant.

The objects of all these societies resemble those set forth in the constitution of the American league:

'(A) To promote and protect the general professional interests of all creators of literary, dramatic or musical material.

'(B) To procure adequate copyright legislation, both international and domestic, and to promote better copyright relations between the United States and other countries.

'(C) To promote fair dealings and to cultivate, establish and maintain harmony, cordial relationship, unity of action and understanding among the members of the League; and between members, on the one hand, and on the other hand, individuals, firms, corporations, associations or organizations who employ them or purchase their material, or with whom they work or have business or other dealings; and to protect the rights of members in that respect.

'(D) To procure better working conditions for its members and payment for their work, commensurate with its value, to correct abuses to which they may be subject, and to bring about harmonious and concerted action by its members in such respects.

'(E) To promote the equitable adjustment of all disputes relating to the professional work of its members.

'(F) To disseminate information as to the rights and interests of its members.

'(G) To establish and enforce standard minimum contracts, and to do any and all other things necessary, proper or desirable to carry into effect or to further any of the foregoing purposes.'

These are all necessary functions, clearly put. In the jurisdiction of the Authors Guild, we may expect to see all of them realized and embodied as a code of fair practices within a century or two. The kittle cattle of the book and magazine trades—

authors, agents, editors, publishers, printers, binders, book clubs, wholesalers, booksellers, advertisers, and even the occasional censor—make any shorter term unlikely. Impatience is not in order. The great-grandchildren of novelists now living may yet see a book or magazine produced by the orderly cooperation of reasonable men.

In the meantime, there is the Authors League. It was incorporated by professional writers in 1912. Except for a small salaried staff (*small* may be applied both ways), its writer-members conduct the democratic affairs of the league, serve on its volunteer committees, make its policies and carry on its negotiations. It is solely an organization conducted by and for writers, in the belief that every improvement in trade conditions will be an improvement for the writer.

The guild has always concerned itself with '(A) the law governing writing and (B) the customs governing writing.' If it had no function but the exchange of information about trade practices, it would still be unique and indispensable. But as a part of its guardian long-term objectives, it is continually at work on specific campaigns in one or another area of the book and magazine field.

Over the years, the guild has been foremost in establishing the practice of recording copyright in the author's name—a notable advance. This in turn be-

came a base for the guild's effort to set up the principle of separate rights, so that each of the 'subsidiary rights' might be bargained for in terms of
the special conditions that govern it, and as a separate property of the author. In these and such other
matters as payment on acceptance for magazine
work, or the payment of accounting royalties to an-
thology contributors, the guild's record stands high.

Since 1926 a minimum basic agreement has been in
force between the Dramatists Guild of the Authors
League and the League of New York Theatres and
other theatrical producers. Just before midcentury,
the publishers of this book and the Authors Guild
successfully negotiated the first minimum basic
agreement in the book contract field. In the history
of relations between American authors and book
publishers, this was an event second in importance
only to the copyright law of 1891. Nor was it a matter of conceding ground already lost. On the contrary, it was mutual ground gained. It signified the
praiseworthy recognition that time and money
might be saved by establishing a common base for
the negotiation of each individual contract. Other
publishers, according to the slowness of their apprehension, might perceive at their leisure that a
man who speaks Iranian and another who speaks
Iraqi will do better if they converse in French.

A novelist may feel that he cannot afford to belong
to the Authors Guild. Actually, he cannot afford not

to. He should regard the modest dues of the guild as a fixed part of his overhead, deductible from taxes. They will come back to him many times in ways he is not even aware of.

The guild is every writer's friend.

12 the agent

The literary agent is a business agent.

Usually he is not, and should not be asked to be, (A) a magician who can produce checks out of a hat; (B) a weird psychologist who can read editors' minds; (C) a literary critic; (D) an instructor in writing; or (E) a man whose function is to provide one dry crying towel after another.

Now and again he may need to be all of these things, to some extent. If he is a good judge of the technical aspects of writing, that will do him and his client no harm. But the novelist must not lean on him in this respect. If he does, he will be wasting his agent's working day. Nor should he expect an agent to tell him how to rewrite a book—even in purely commercial terms. A good agent will often know more about such current terms and conditions than the writer. But this does not mean he is an oracle. The circumstances are such that even the best agent can deal only in limited probabilities. In all these matters, however, the novelist should be open to advice and willing to reflect on it.

The agent's business is business. In regard to his client, his function is (A) to offer for sale or lease, or otherwise promote, the rights to his client's literary work; (B) to advance and promote his client's future literary services; (C) in consultation with his client, and always with his client's agreement obtained in advance, to arrange terms, negotiate contracts, accept sums payable to the client, and otherwise guard and advance his client's interests. For these services he is entitled to a standard fee of ten per cent of the sums received by the author, deductible in advance.

The Authors Guild will help any professional writer to choose a reputable agent. It will not advise him as to the choice between one reputable agent and another.

The good agent will be a lion in defense of his author's interests and a cooing dove when the case demands it. Like the actors' agent, he must work with the negotiable effects of personality and convert them somehow into commercial terms. Sometimes this will not be difficult. At other times it may call for the diplomacy of a Talleyrand.

The novelist should be aware that an agent thinks of his work primarily as a property, a commodity. If he did not do this, he could not place it. Moreover, this placement is a business transaction; and no transaction is a deal until it is closed. Thus, on occasion, the agent may wish to close a deal on the

best available terms, like any business man; but the
novelist may consider some literary aspect important enough to require holding the negotiations
open—or even, in extreme cases, breaking them off.
(We need hardly point out that no case is 'extreme'
until every available alternative has been tried.)

In any event, the novelist must make his own literary terms, through his agent. The agent is not to
be held responsible for the conditions that obtain.
He did not make them; and it may be that he is doing his best to help improve them. Or, like other
business men, he may prefer to work with a fixed
status quo. In any case, the novelist must decide
what he will or will not do—whether he will rewrite
or condense for a magazine, and whether he will
cut his book or take out the bad little words for a
reprint edition. He should not allow his judgment
to be overawed by the sleight-of-hand assurance of
business men or editors, or the prestige of a 'big
publisher,' or of New York. Very few editors carry
the winged thunderbolts of Zeus; and wisdom does
not make her exclusive perch on the mooring mast
of the Empire State Building.

The novelist should remind himself that every literary decision of his will help to break or establish
those commercial customs under which his fellow
writers must work.

He should not forget that he owes certain obligations to his agent. The first and last of these is fair

dealing on terms of mutual confidence. In commercial matters, he should not act without consulting his agent; and he should not be niggardly about paying his agent's fee even in cases where he himself may have had a large part in closing a transaction.

The beginning novelist need not be in too much of a hurry about getting himself an agent. Unless something extraordinary happens, he will have very little business to transact. He and his agent may not be worth each other's time. But he should be a member of the Authors Guild, if he is eligible, and refer all contracts and agreements to the guild before he signs them.

The agent displays his greatest usefulness as a guide through the jungle of 'subsidiary rights.' Here he is often indispensable. These rights, which comprise such matters as book or magazine reprints, foreign publication, translation, dramatic and radio, screen or television licensing, require a specialist's knowledge of immediate conditions, contracts and legal difficulties. The Authors Guild may be as well, or better, informed than any single agency. But the guild can hardly be expected to conduct each of its members through each step of a thousand diverse transactions.

Here, as elsewhere, the guild and the agent have complementary functions. They are necessary to each other; and both are necessary to the novelist.

The nearest analogy, perhaps, is the example of the musicians' union and the musician's agent.

An agent will often make an excellent friend.

13 the publisher

Any damn fool, as Mark Twain is reported to have said, can write a book, and any damn fool can read one, but it takes a *man* to sell it. The publisher— with his confederates, the salesman, the advertising man, the wholesaler, and the bookseller—is that man.

A publisher is just like anybody else, only smarter.

To the author, he resembles one of those two-faced father gods of mythology, Shiva or Viracocha, whose aspect is simultaneously benevolent and malign.

Women writers purr in the warmth of his charm, only to find out later that he has inserted a very awkward clause in their contracts. Being women, they forgive this, but reserve it for later use. Male writers tend to become indignant and to denounce the publisher for that very skill in business which should benefit them in the end, if they are wise enough to take advantage of it.

Publishers are not necessarily either philanthropists or rogues. Likewise they are usually neither lordly magnates nor cringing beggars. As a working hypothesis, regard them as ordinary human beings trying to earn their living at an unusually difficult occupation.' [45]

Publishers merge, consolidate, or absorb each other, according to the laws that govern the functions of elementary organisms. But it is axiomatic in the trade that they seldom fail.

Writers sometimes do.

In the field of true venture capital, the book publisher is almost the last man left on the corner. No one has yet worked out a way to insure him—or the author—against the failure of a book. Like the author, he is naked to all the winds of trade; but his corner is a little less exposed.

In this respect he can be compared only with the ladies' garment manufacturer. Both deal in a unique unit of merchandise—a presumably limited number of copies of a particular model in this season's line—and it is hardly remarkable that their methods, at the worst, should sometimes display an unpleasant similarity.

What *is* remarkable, however, is that so many publishers should so often evince a superior notion of cultural and social responsibility. (This 'self-transcendence' is not entirely altruism. The competition is very stiff.) Time and again, a publisher will

bring out a valuable book that is evidently not going to sell much, and back it with the heat of personal and hard-cash evangelism. We need only
compare this with the usual behavior of motion-
picture and radio producers to glimpse its exem-
plary quality.

By and large, the book publisher shows a relatively
high degree of professional integrity; and he will
often match this with a remarkable freedom of
judgment. Such virtue produces its own dividends.
These are not often excessively financial; but the
publisher is likely to be a happier and less ulcerous
man than his opposite number in advertising or
radio or motion pictures. Moreover, his prestige is
higher, or at least of a choicer kind.

In the aggregate scale of business, the book trade
is a very small operation; and there is a touch of
gallantry about its more or less habitual defiance of
the standards imposed by the Goliaths of radio, the
popular magazines, the motion pictures, and so on.
If we are looking for free speech at its freest, we
must usually go to the book publisher. Even here,
there is some tendency toward commercial soften-
ing—not in ideas, but in the picayune and transient
aspects of morals. In this respect, the lies of the
book trade threaten only its own standards. They
are white indeed if we set them against the traditional and systematic evasions of the other public
media.

The publisher is bedeviled with three of the most intransigeant factors any business must deal with: (A) a reading public which, by and large, does not care to read if there is anything else to do; (B) a manufacturing and merchandising system so medieval that many readers cannot afford to buy new books, and most booksellers find it indecently hard to make a living; and (C) the author, who lays the golden egg, and who is sometimes a goose.

What the novelist needs to know is that his interests are never quite identical with those of the publisher, nor yet completely antithetic. Sometimes they are very nearly identical, as in the choice of a type face or even the advertising copy for his book. Sometimes they are almost entirely opposed, as in negotiating the financial clauses of a contract. But there will always be a margin of accommodation.

Almost nothing—short of complete economic idiocy and a good book every six months—will make a novelist so welcome in his publisher's office as a little knowledge of protocol in these matters. He should try to learn the relative degree of self-interest or accommodation called for at each point on the scale.

If the publisher's usually admirable tact must strain to meet a generalized suspicion extending to such matters as the quality of paper in a dust wrapper, it may be bad for his character. If he wins too many easy victories, that will be bad for him too. He may become cynical or wily. Every decent-minded novelist will wish to save him from this fate.

Publishing is a business conducted with punctilio, in beautiful surroundings, and usually with gloves on. If the novelist has no gloves, he may borrow an old pair from his publisher.

Once these things are understood, a publisher will often make an excellent friend.

14 the editor

The publisher's editor has two chief functions in regard to the writer: (A) to prepare his novel for the printer, and to see that it is printed in good order; (B) to suggest or advise small emendations or improvements in punctuation, spelling, syntax, hyperbaton—anything, in fact, from the choice of a title to the usage of the nouns of multitude.

If he is forced to take on other duties, this means (A) that the publisher, for literary, commercial or other reasons, hopes to have certain changes made in the book; or (B) that the writer does not know his job, or has not done it thoroughly. The more the writer has done, and the better he has done it, the less will the publisher's editor be required to do.

Very often the editor is a patient, bright, discrimi-
nating man, skilled in his profession, inordinately
tactful, and frequently overworked. All too often,
however, he has no choice but to play wet nurse,
technical adviser, father substitute, psychiatrist
and butcher to the novelist. The editor's office fills
with a hard whine of disputation like the noise of a
power saw going into a teakwood log. The editor
wishes he had not been born and the writer is convinced that he should not have been.

Sometimes there are explanatory circumstances.
Sometimes, too, the publisher may wish to make
commercial changes, and the editor must act as his
negotiator. This is a mistake, in general, unless the
book is purely commercial in the first place. If the
publisher requires a book written to order he
should hire an employee to do it. A good writer
can't serve two masters, and the sense of being his
own master is as vital to his work as the air he
breathes.

Far too often, however, the hurt feelings in the
editor's office betray a default of function by the
writer. He has not done his job well enough, and
the editor must try to do it for him. This is scan-
dalous. A man should do his own hard work. He
should not push it off on someone else. Every writer
who turns in a foul manuscript demeans his professional pride and the repute of every other writer.

Writing a novel is a one-man job—the novelist's.

Editing a novel for publication is a one-man job—the editor's.

They are cooperative. They need not conflict.

An editor will often make an excellent friend.

15 the reviewer or critic

'Kill the dog,' said Goethe, 'he is a reviewer.'

Or the opposite counsel: bear wrongs patiently.

The literary code of manners enjoins that the novelist shall make no reply to the reviewer or critic, except perhaps in the case of a serious factual error.

If this were not so, the best fighter or the best dialectician would be per se the best novelist or the best critic. This might take years to prove and would certainly waste everybody's time.

In such matters an arbitrary code is necessary. The reviewer or critic needs the greatest possible freedom in order to arrive at a fair estimate of a book, whether as a work of literature, an article or commerce, or both. This freedom must be inviolable.

The critic is, and should be, limited in one essential respect. If he discusses the author instead of the book—if he becomes personal, that is—he lays him-

self open to the same kind of action he would encounter in any comparable human situation: a libel
suit, or a punch in the nose.

Both are unlikely, though salutary as an occasional
corrective in literary groups, where manners may
tend to take on the unbridled feminine malicious-
ness of a girls' school on a picnic.

The novelist should remember that his book is often
treated a good deal better than it deserves.

In private, of course, he may say what he thinks,
and usually does. His wife, close relatives, and
friends should listen with becoming sympathy
while he praises the acumen of a favorable critic
or denounces the ancestors of a hostile one.

All critics who do not like his book are hostile
critics.

There have been known instances, however, in
which a novelist has agreed with a critic who did
not like his book, or disagreed with a critic who did.
A professional novelist may dislike being praised
for the wrong reasons almost as much as he dislikes
being taken to task for not doing something he had
never intended to do.

When he has reached a certain point in his career,
he will care only for the opinions of a few fellow

professionals and a half-dozen reviewers or critics whose judgment he regards as sound. At that point he is willing to leave the clutch of reviewers to his publisher. But in the beginning, he walks like a naked child among the wolves.

Certain critics find it necessary to ignore the novelist's performance and intention in order to concentrate on the main object: their own critical reputations.

Others will cheerfully discount their reputations in defense of an unpopular book they consider good.

'When a man says you are a horse, laugh at him; when two men assert it, give it a thought; and when three men say you are a horse, you had better go and buy a saddle for yourself.' [37]

It may be well to remember that the critic or reviewer is likely to be even more poorly paid than the novelist.

Critics are presumably human, though the evidence is not yet conclusive.

16 the reader

A reader should be loved and cared for like a motherless child.

17 the rewards: public and private

There are moments when every novelist would deny on his oath that he ever got an instant of pleasure or satisfaction out of writing. But of course it is not true, and he knows it is not.

The publication of his first book—at least until the reviews begin to come in—will be an occasion warm with bells and flowers. The season is always spring. For a week or two, at least, he will be able to think well of himself. Though he no longer has any real business there, he will open the door of his publisher's office like a man sure of his welcome. He will see his name, even his picture, in the newspapers; and these evidences of public notice will take some of the sting out of the hard or lukewarm words that go with them. His friends will smile at him, mercifully reserving judgment for a later occasion. People he does not know will ask him to parties.

The best of it is that he will make new friends—people brought to him by his book, or he to them. If they have really liked it, it will be a guarantee between him and them. They will nod and say: Yes, it is good.

Later, if some book of his catches on, the novelist may even become a minor celebrity for a while. If he is a fool, or not very hard-headed, he may be taken in. He will be seen in fashionable places, and cultivate a liking to be seen. He will not be aware that most of this has very little to do with the integrity of his work. It is a public deference paid to a man who has—in a small way, at least—vindicated the American legend. He has shown himself capable of earning presumably large sums of money in ways that other people would like to be able to emulate. There is some envy in this deference, and both are founded on a cultivated illusion.

He will be asked to speak, to do his part in radio or television, or to give his opinions on books and the state of the world. If he is a professional, he will do these things, but he will hardly notice them. They mean nothing but more work for him. He knows that such nonsense is fleeting. He does it to please his publisher and other friends, or because he feels it may help his book a little.

There is sometimes, even, a respectable amount of money. He does not change his way of life because of that. He knows better. But for a month, or six months, the novelist may imagine that he can live a little more freely, that he has got over the hump. Then things shut down again.

In the end, there is nothing, no happiness, but that happiness he finds for whole hours in the doing of the thing itself. Each time it surprises him. It comes unbelievably, like some gentle, limpid gift, from

what quarter he does not know. He hardly welcomes it. He allows it to take possession of him; and
the work flows like the brook of his childhood,
where the watercress and the skunk cabbage made
a margin for the clear stream. He has only to stand
on the little bridge and watch it move under his
eye.

'He values it,' said Henry James, 'all sublimely and
perhaps a little fatuously, for itself — as the great extension, great beyond all others, of experience and
of consciousness; with the toil and trouble a mere
sun-cast shadow that falls, shifts and vanishes, the
result of his living in so large a light. . . . He en-
joys it, so to speak, without a tax; the effort of
labour involved, the torment of expression, of which
we have heard in our time so much, being after all
but the last refinement of his privilege. It may leave
him weary and worn; but how, after his fashion, he
will have lived!' [26]

If he has done his work, the best day's work he is
capable of, he can get up from the table with a
sense of virtue so quiet and deep that it will speak
to everyone around him. For an hour or two, he is
like a saint in the house. The depth of his exhausted
joy has room for all the pleasure of others. He is the
best listener in the world; and he will sleep like a
child who does not know the meaning of trouble.

Sometimes he will take down a book he wrote a
dozen years ago. It is no longer his. He has lost all

connection with it. But as he reads, his eyebrows go up. Did I do that? he thinks. So long ago? It isn't so bad. That page there—that night on the wharf. How young I was. And how much I could hope.

As long as he lives, the announcement of each new book is like a letter to his friends. Look, it says. I am alive. I have made a little story for you. See if it does not speak of something we hold in common, the sad or ridiculous history of a person or a time. Do you remember New York when the awnings of the sidewalk cafés come out? Were you lost too that cold winter in the Thirties? Do you remember Georgia in the spring, and the landfall at the Farallones, and Loveland Pass in the snow? Can you think of a time in which we will be happy again? See. Here it is. I made it for you.

references

1 ALLEN, WALTER, ed. *The Writer on His Art.*

1A AUTHORS GUILD. HULL, HELEN, ed. *The Writer's Book.*

1B BARNHART, CLARENCE L., ed. *The American College Dictionary.*

2 BOSANQUET, THEODORA. *Henry James at Work.*

3 BURKE, KENNETH. *Counter-Statement.*

4 —— *Attitudes toward History.*

5 CANNON, WALTER B. *The Way of An Investigator.*

6 COMMANVILLE, CAROLINE. *Intimate Remembrances of Gustave Flaubert.*

7 COMPTON-BURNETT, I. *Two Worlds and Their Ways.*

8 —— *Brothers and Sisters.*

9 DAICHES, DAVID. *A Study of Literature for Readers and Critics.*

9A DEVOTO, BERNARD. *Mark Twain at Work.*

10 DEWEY, JOHN. *Art As Experience.*

11 DOWNEY, JUNE E. *Creative Imagination.*

12 FERNANDEZ, RAMON. *Messages.* Translated from the French by Montgomery Belgion.

13 FITZGERALD, F. SCOTT. *The Great Gatsby.*

14 FLAUBERT, GUSTAVE. *Correspondence.*

15 GALTON, FRANCIS. *Inquiries Into Human Faculty.*

16 GILES, HERBERT A. *A History of Chinese Literature.*

17 GOWEN, HERBERT H. *A History of Indian Literature.*

18 GREEN, HENRY. *Concluding.*

19 —— *Loving.*

20 —— *Party-Going.*

21 HADAMARD, JACQUES. *An Essay on The Psychology of Invention in The Mathematical Field.*

22 HARRISON, JANE. *Ancient Art and Ritual.*

23 HERODOTUS. *The Persian Wars.* Translated by George Rawlinson.

24 HOMER. *The Odyssey.* Translated by E. V. Rieu.

25 HYMAN, STANLEY EDGAR. *The Armed Vision.*

26 JAMES, HENRY. *The Art of the Novel.*

27 —— *Partial Portraits.*

28 —— *Essays in London and Elsewhere.*

29 KOESTLER, ARTHUR. *Insight and Outlook.*

30 LOWES, JOHN LIVINGSTON. *The Road to Xanadu.*

31 LUBBOCK, PERCY. *The Craft of Fiction.*

32 LUCIAN OF SAMOSATA. *The True History.* Translated by H. W. and F. G. Fowler.

33 MALLEA, EDUARDO. *The Bay of Silence.* Translated from the Spanish by Stuart Edgar Grummon.

34 MATTHIESSEN, F. O., and MURDOCK, KENNETH B., ed. *The Notebooks of Henry James.*

35 POLNER, TIKHON. *Tolstoy and His Wife.* Translated by Nicholas Wreden.

35A PRESCOTT, FREDERICK CLARKE. *The Poetic Mind.*

36 READ, HERBERT. *Education Through Art.*

37 REIK, THEODOR. *Listening With the Third Ear.*

38 RICHARDS, I. A. *Coleridge on Imagination.*

39 ROMAINS, JULES. *Men of Good Will.*

40 SAINTSBURY, GEORGE. *A Short History of French Literature.*

41 —— *The English Novel.*

42 SARTRE, JEAN-PAUL. *The Psychology of Imagination.*

43 STARKIE, ENID. *Arthur Rimbaud.*

44 THOMSON, J. A. K. *The Classical Background of English Literature.*

45 UNWIN, SIR STANLEY, LL.D. *The Truth About Publishing.*

46 VINCENT, HOWARD P. *The Trying-Out of Moby-Dick.*

47 WELEK, RENÉ and WARREN, AUSTIN. *Theory of Literature.*

47A WESCOTT, GLENWAY. *The Pilgrim Hawk.*

48 WHARTON, EDITH. *A Backward Glance.*

49 WHITEHEAD, ALFRED NORTH. *Science and the Modern World.*

50 WITTENBERG, PHILIP. *The Protection and Marketing of Literary Property.*

51 WOOLF, VIRGINIA. *The Moment and Other Essays.*

52 —— *Mrs. Dalloway.* Introduction to the Modern Library edition.

53 ZWEIG, STEFAN. *Balzac.* Translated by William and Dorothy Rose.